HAYES PRESS

GROWING DISCIPLES

A BIBLE STUDY COURSE FOR FOLLOWERS OF JESUS

HAYES
PRESS Christian Publisher

First edition

This book was professionally typeset on Reedsy.
Find out more at reedsy.com

Contents

Preface

If you are a new disciple of the Lord Jesus, or one who wishes to learn the basic teaching of the Bible for disciples, then this course is for you. The Bible describes you as a "baby in Christ", someone who needs to be fed and nourished by someone else so that you may grow into full maturity: "Like newborn babies, crave pure spiritual milk, so that by it you may grow up in your salvation (1 Peter 2:2). This course assumes that you are a born-again Christian (see John 3), although the assurance of that salvation is dealt with in Session 2. It also assumes you want to be a disciple who is continuously learning about Christ and being obedient to him.

The course consists of 23 sessions, split between doctrinal and practical topics. It is intended to be taught in either of two ways: in a group situation with a facilitator who will also lead the group through the material in the Topic Overview (each session is expected to take about 90 minutes), or by self-study at your own pace. In both cases, you will need your own Bible, preferably an NIV, NKJV, ESV or NASB translation. In the case of self-study, suggested answers to the Discussion Questions in each session are at the back of the book - no cheating! For facilitated sessions, the following 90-minute timeline is suggested:

1. Take up the Review Questions from the previous session (15 min.)
2. Discuss the Assignment from the previous session (10 min.)
3. Answer any questions about the Advance Reading (5 min.)
4. Go over the Topic Overview (with visual aids) (30 min.)
5. Learn the Memory Verse together (5 min.)
6. Discuss some or all of the Discussion Questions in one group or in small

groups. (20 min.)

7. Give the Assignment and Advance Reading for the following session (5 min.)

Some of the material may possibly seem very elementary depending on your prior knowledge, and on your age and capacity. Others may find it more difficult and need extra help. It is impossible for each session to cover its topic in great depth – please see the back of the book for a list of additional study books and booklets available from Hayes Press (many are available for download at no charge at www.churchesofgod.info).

1

DISCIPLESHIP

OBJECTIVE

1. To understand that progressively learning about and applying the teaching of Christ from the Word of God should be the goal and life-work of every believer in Christ. 2. To stimulate the desire and willingness to be a disciple of the Lord Jesus.

ADVANCE READING

Read the following Scriptures and briefly summarize each one: 1. Matthew 28:18-20; 2. John 8:31,32; 3. Luke 6:40; 4. Luke 14:26-33.

TOPIC OVERVIEW

a) Who is a disciple of the Lord Jesus?

A disciple is a follower of someone else. We are disciples of the Lord Jesus Christ. He is our leader. A prerequisite of being a disciple is to have accepted Jesus Christ as your personal Saviour through faith. A disciple is a student. He follows in order to learn and, in doing so, learns more about following.

See Luke 6:40. Christ uses the Holy Spirit, who indwells us because we are believers in Christ, to teach us about Him. The goal of discipleship is to be well-pleasing to God. This involves an on-going process of constant renewal - of being changed to be more like Christ Himself (Colossians 3:10; Romans 8:29).

b) What did the Lord Jesus say a disciple was?

Jesus said 'If you hold to my teaching, you are really my disciples' (John 8:31). What does this mean?

- "if you hold" - means: learning, understanding and applying to my life; it is a condition which is my responsibility;
- "my teaching" - Jesus' teaching; not teachings (plural)- there are many elements but it is one unified teaching; it must be taken as a whole; there are no substitutes or options;
- "my disciples" - Jesus' own disciples; an identification with Jesus, based on a personal relationship with Him.

c) What are the characteristics of a disciple?

i) Luke 14:26-33:

- verse 26 - hates (meaning loves less than) family and own life (see Matthew 10:37);
- verse 27 - carries own cross (the sacrifices and reproach), and follows Jesus;
- verse 33 - the Lord Jesus is given priority over everything else in my life.

ii) John 14:21 - knows Christ's commands and obeys them.

iii) Luke 9:23 - denies oneself; takes up cross daily, follows Christ.

d) What are the actions of a disciple?

- John 8:31 – holding to Jesus' teaching; that is, doing it consistently;
- John 13:34,35 – loving my "brother and sister" is evidence to others that we are disciples of Christ;
- John 15:8 – bearing fruit (using the analogy of a vine), as evidence of discipleship.

e) What is the cost of being a disciple?

Read the story of Carla:

> *Haunting strains of flute music filtered out onto the city street. The melody was so beautiful that for the moment the roar of the traffic and sounds of kids on the corner ceased to register in Carla's ears. All she could hear was the sweet music coming from Apartment 2B. That was where Mrs. Rosinee lived. She was the woman who was playing the haunting music. She was the woman Carla wanted to be like. As the music continued, Carla recalled the conversation she had with Mrs. Rosinee during Carla's music lesson that morning. Carla had told her teacher that someday she wanted to be as good a flute player as she was.*

> *Carla had expected Mrs. Rosinee to be glad that Carla wanted to play well, and that she would give her a few extra pieces to practise. Carla hadn't expected the kind of response she had received. Instead of handing Carla extra music, Mrs. Rosinee had said, "Carla, you have the potential to be a great flautist. But not everyone who has potential succeeds. If you truly want to become great, you must give up all activities except your schoolwork; you must spend time with me daily learning my techniques; you must practise diligently; and above all you must do exactly what I say. I do not want you to decide today whether you are willing to do all this. You must think seriously about what it will cost you to make this choice. Next week, at your lesson, you can tell me your*

3

decision."

A loud honk jarred Carla back to the activity of the city street. She looked at the groups of kids laughing on the corner. She knew if she accepted Mrs. Rosinee's challenge, she would be spending no time with them. But as she looked longingly at the kids, the strains of the flute echoed in her mind. Carla Blanchard knew what her choice must be."

Discuss the costs involved in her being a musician. Compare these with the rewards (see Luke 14:25-33; Matthew 10:16-20; 10:21-23; 34-39; 16:24-28).

f) How does a disciple grow?

Read the story of Dennis: Techumseh, Ontario, Canada - 1960.

A shocking story begins to unfold. Fifteen year-old Dennis Donaldson knocks on his neighbour's door. The neighbour calls the police. Why? Was Dennis a hoodlum trying to attack the neighbour? No, Dennis was no hoodlum. Though Dennis was 15, he was only three feet, eleven inches tall and weighed only 44 pounds. And the reason the neighbour called the police was, though the Donaldsons had lived near him a long time, the neighbour hadn't known the boy existed.

Entering the Donaldson's home, the police found not only Dennis but two sisters, Bonnie, 18, and Carrie, 13. Bonnie was four feet, two inches tall and weighed 55 pounds. Carrie was three feet, two inches and weighed 29 pounds. The children had spent 11 years shut in a playroom. Television had kept them in touch with what was going on in the world. And an older sister taught them to read. Why had they been shut away? Various reasons were suggested. One possibility was because the family had six children (three had been allowed to grow up normally) and they could not find a place to live. So the parents had hidden three of the children.

Another possibility was that the three children had something wrong with them and the mother was hiding them so that people would not laugh at them. In any case, the children had had far from a normal existence. Though they had been fed and clothed, they had become physically stunted and emotionally damaged. Tests showed that the teenagers were eight years behind children their own ages. What caused the stunting? It could have been a medical problem. Or, they could have become stunted because of their environment. In either case, the children had been seriously deprived. Though they had received some elements which had contributed to their growth, they had not received others. And this deprivation would affect them for the rest of their lives.

What elements of physical and emotional growth did the children miss out on? Compare these with elements of spiritual growth.

Dennis's Problems

Physical Isolation, No Fresh Air, No schooling, No Social Interaction, No Vision

Spiritual Elements of Growth

Scripture Reading, Prayer, Fellowship, Witnessing, Obedience

g) Disciples are made (not born)!

Matthew 28:19,20: The Lord's apostles were instructed to (a) go and make disciples, (b) baptize them, (c) teach them to obey all of Jesus' teaching. Note the importance of the sequence. How long does it take to make a disciple? It is a life-long, continuous process.

REVIEW QUESTIONS

1. What is a prerequisite to being a disciple of the Lord Jesus?
2. Who is a disciple of the Lord Jesus?
3. What characterizes a disciple of Christ?
4. Name as many actions as you can which a disciple of Christ should be doing.
5. How does one follow the Lord Jesus?
6. What is the cost of being a disciple?
7. How does a disciple grow?
8. Are disciples born or made?
9. Name some of the commands of the Lord Jesus (See Appendix A).

MEMORY VERSE

Luke 9:23 - "If anyone would come after me, he must deny himself and take up his cross daily and follow me."

DISCUSSION QUESTIONS

1. What methods did Jesus use to convey His teaching?
2. How do you find out about, and apply to your life, the teaching of the Lord Jesus?
3. What is the cross that Jesus said we must take up and carry daily, in Luke 14:27? How do you do that?
4. Is discipleship a matter of internal attitudes, knowledge or external actions? (Explain)
5. What is the practical difference between accepting Christ as your Saviour, and being a disciple with Christ as your Lord?
6. What are the rewards, now and in the future, of being a disciple of Christ?
7. What is the evidence of lack of spiritual growth in a person?
8. How is a disciple made?
9. Refer to Appendix A, which is a list of references of the commandments

of the Lord. There are 80, based on this classification, with over 600 New Testament references. Which ones are referred to most frequently? Which ones are you not familiar with?

ASSIGNMENT

Each day until the next session, select a commandment of the Lord from Appendix A, read all the related Scriptures, and make a plan of action as to how to carry it out.

2

THE REALITY OF SALVATION

OBJECTIVES

1. To understand the extent of what God did to us at the time of our salvation.
2. To be convinced that our salvation is permanent and cannot be lost.

ADVANCE READING

Read the following Scriptures and write a brief summary of the main point of each: 1 Peter 3:18; 2. Romans 5; 3. Ephesians 2:1-10; 4. John 10:25-30

TOPIC OVERVIEW

Very few people fully realize, at the moment that they receive salvation, all that God is doing for and to them at that particular time. Understanding the extent of God's work of salvation in us is something that we can only really begin to appreciate afterwards. The purpose of this session is to understand some of what God accomplished in you in your salvation, and also to realize that it is permanent and can never be lost.

a) Why is salvation necessary?

Everyone has a sinful nature. We were born with it, and inherited it through our parents, from the first man Adam (see Psalm 51:5; Romans 5:12). We cannot change this. As a result of it, we all commit acts of sin - thoughts, words, actions that are contrary to God. We are incapable of correcting this or of totally reforming ourselves. How does Ephesians 2:1,2 describe our condition before we were saved? We were 'dead in your transgressions and sins.'

b) What did it require to save you?

God, being totally righteous, cannot overlook sin of any kind. The penalty for it must be paid in every case to atone for it, and the penalty is death (Romans 6:23)! Therefore - it either requires that we pay this penalty for our own sins, or else an acceptable substitute must do so. Otherwise, God's righteousness would be compromised.Romans 3:26 says that God justified us (made us righteous) and yet remained righteous Himself by requiring the penalty to be borne by someone else. Christ's death on the cross was the sacrifice of a sinless man on behalf of all other members of the human race. He, the Son of God from heaven, took on human nature (without giving up His divine nature) so that He could represent the entire human race and so be their substitute. He himself had to be sinless so that His death would be for others, and not be required for His own sin.

What does Ephesians 2:8 say about God's part and our part in our salvation? God's part: God, in His grace, gave us salvation as a gift. Our part: we accepted it by faith! What was required of you in order to receive this gift of salvation, according to Acts 20:21? Repentance and faith. What is a definition of 'the grace of God'? God acting in our best interests despite the fact that we did not deserve it!

c) Keeping your salvation

You can never lose your salvation. It is eternally guaranteed by God, who seals us with His Holy Spirit (Ephesians 1:13). Keeping your salvation is the work of Christ, and doesn't depend on what you do. What assurance of this does John 10:28 give you - "I give them eternal life, and they shall never perish"? If you ever begin to doubt that you are eternally saved, remember John 10:28. Also, go back to the verses in the Bible that originally showed you that you were saved, and read them again. Examples: John 3:16; John 5:24; Acts 16:31; Romans 10:9; Ephesians 2:8.

Some people mistakenly believe that they can lose their salvation - either by sinning, or else by not continuing to believe in Christ. It's called the 'falling away doctrine.' It is based on Scriptures such as Hebrews 6:4-6; but these verses refer to our service and fellowship with God, not to our eternal salvation.

d) From what are you saved?

There are 3 tenses, or time frames, to our salvation:

- when we first put faith in Christ, we were saved once for all from the **penalty** of our sins. We shall never have to bear that penalty (see Romans 8:1);
- we are now given the opportunity, through the Holy Spirit, to be saved day by day from the **power** of sin in our lives (see Philippians 2:12);
- we are assured that, in the future when Christ returns to the air, we will be saved finally from the **presence** of all sin (see Romans 13:11).

Remember: Penalty - Power - Presence.

e) How were you changed?

Listed below are 8 ways in which God permanently changed you when you were saved:

1) You were **REGENERATED** - that is, 'born again.' From being dead in sins to God, you were made alive to God (Romans 6:11). How is this life described in John 3:16? Eternal. What did you become? (John 1:12,13) - a child of God; everyone is the 'offspring' of God, as Acts 17:28 shows, but only believers in Christ are children of God and able to call God their Father.

2) You were **FORGIVEN** - that is, God no longer holds you accountable for your sins, since Christ has already borne all the punishment, and you have acknowledged that He has done so for you. How does Ephesians 1:7 describe this? Our forgiveness by God is the result of Christ redeeming us, at the cost of His blood, which He did in grace.

3) You were **JUSTIFIED** - that is, you have been judged by God to be 'not guilty', and therefore righteous. What did it cost Christ to accomplish this, according to Romans 5:9,18,19? His blood; one act of righteousness; obedience.

4) You were **RECONCILED** - that is, you were brought back from being estranged and at enmity with God, to being at peace with Him. What does Colossians 1:20-22 say about this? Previously we were enemies in our minds to God because of our evil behaviour; but Christ's death has taken that barrier away.

5) You were **REDEEMED** - that is, purchased from sin and Satan at the price of Christ's death. As a result, you now belong to Him as His possession. How does 1 Corinthians 6:19,20 describe it? You are not your own; you were bought at a price.

6) You were **BAPTIZED** in the Holy Spirit into 'the Church the Body of Christ',

which consists of all believers in Christ (see 1 Corinthians 12:13). This is quite distinct from being baptized in water as a disciple, which should follow salvation.

7) You were **SANCTIFIED** - that is, made holy. This means to be cleansed and set apart totally for God. People who have been sanctified are referred to in the Bible as 'saints.' What do 1 Corinthians 6:11 and Hebrews 10:10 say about this? You used to be wicked but you have been sanctified once for all by the sacrifice of Christ's body.

8) You were **INDWELT** - that is, by the Holy Spirit of God as the permanent presence of God within you. This makes you a 'temple' of God, since wherever God lives is a temple (or sanctuary). How does 1 Corinthians 6:19 refer to this? Your body is a temple; the Holy Spirit from God is in you.

REVIEW QUESTIONS

1. Why did you need to be saved?
2. What did it require to save you?
3. What did you have to do to receive this salvation?
4. What should you do if you ever doubt you are saved?
5. Can you ever lose your salvation?
6. What are you saved from?
7. What changes did God make in you when you were saved?

MEMORY VERSE

Romans 8:1 - "Therefore, there is now no condemnation for those who are in Christ Jesus."

DISCUSSION QUESTIONS

1. What is the grace of God?
2. Explain how there was no other way for God to achieve our salvation.
3. What does it mean to be justified?
4. What does it mean to be sanctified?
5. What is the result of not knowing about, or not accepting this salvation?
6. "If I was saved a long time ago but have done nothing for God since then, how do I know that I am still saved?"

ASSIGNMENT

Following are some commonly-held misconceptions about salvation. From the following Scriptures (and perhaps others) show how they are incorrect:

1. 'just believing is too easy; there must be more to it.'
2. 'everyone will be saved; a God of love would not punish anyone in hell.'
3. 'if I live a good life, I'll be saved.'
4. 'I have to be baptized (or 'confirmed') to be saved.'

Scriptures: Isaiah 64:6; John 3:36; John 8:21; Acts 16:31; Romans 6:23; Ephesians 2:8,9; 1 Peter 3:21

3

WATER BAPTISM

OBJECTIVES

1. To understand the significance of baptism for believers. 2. To appreciate the importance of being baptized.

ADVANCE READING

Read the following Scriptures and write a short statement giving the main point of each: 1. Matthew 28:18-20; 2. Acts 2:41; 3. Acts 8:35-39; 4. Acts 10:47,48; 5. Acts 16:30-33; 6. Acts 19:3-5; 7. Romans 6:3-5; 8. 1 Peter 3:20,21

TOPIC OVERVIEW

a) What is baptism?

The word 'baptism' is used with different meanings in Scripture. The primary ones in the New Testament are:

- John's baptism in water - e.g. Matthew 3:5,6; Acts 19:4. This was for Jews, to demonstrate their repentance from Israel's sin, to prepare themselves for the coming of the Christ;

- baptism in the Holy Spirit - e.g. John 1:33; 1 Corinthians 12:13. This is a spiritual baptism (not with water) whereby, at salvation, Christ baptizes the believer in the Holy Spirit into the Church the Body of Christ (See Session 16). This happens automatically to every believer;
- believers' baptism in water - e.g. Matthew 28:20; Acts 2:41. This is immersion in water by a believer in Christ as an act of obedience in demonstration of a commitment to be a disciple of the Lord Jesus Christ. It is this baptism that is the subject of this session.

b) Who is baptism for?

Baptism is for believers in Christ. It is not required for their salvation, but it should follow salvation in the case of all believers. See, for example, the following instances:

- Acts 2:41 - "Those who accepted his message";
- Acts 8:12 - "when they believed Philip";
- Acts 9:18 - "Immediately";
- Acts 10:47 – "Can anyone";
- Acts 16:14,15 – "The Lord opened her heart".

Some people believe that baptism is for:

- infants - as a commitment by the parents to bring up the children in a godly way, or to ensure the child's access to the kingdom of God. However, all scriptural examples of water baptism are of mature believers who made the decision for themselves;
- entire families (households) - this is sometimes based on the case of Lydia (Acts 16:15) or the jailor (Acts 16:33) where entire families were baptized at the same time. However, in both cases, it is clear that the entire households heard the gospel and believed it before being baptized.

c) How does baptism take place?

Baptism comes from the Greek word 'baptizo', which means 'to immerse.' Thus baptism means to dip or immerse. According to Scripture, the immersion is in water. The water is not 'holy' water, but ordinary. That believers' baptism involves immersion in water is clear from the case of the Ethiopian eunuch in Acts 8:38,39: "Then both Philip and the eunuch went down into the water and Philip baptised him. When they came up out of the water ..." Thus, sprinkling water on a child (or anyone else) does not constitute scriptural baptism.

d) Baptism into what?

In Acts 19:3 (RV), Paul asked the disciples at Ephesus, "Into what then were ye baptized?" They replied: "Into John's baptism." Since this was not believers' baptism, Paul instructed them to be baptized again "into the name of the Lord Jesus." It is therefore important into what a believer is baptized, and what significance is understood by that. The full expression is given to us in the Lord's first commandment to baptize disciples in Matthew 28:19 (RV): "baptizing them into the name of the Father and of the Son and of the Holy Ghost." Baptism into this name acknowledges the deity of the Lord Jesus - as Son of God - and His authority.

e) The significance of believers' baptism

Romans 6:4,5 explains that immersion in water symbolizes burial into death - the death of the old life of self, and that rising out of the water symbolizes resurrection into new life - a life following Christ as leader.

There is an Old Testament illustration of this in 1 Corinthians 10:2. The Israelites were all "baptised into Moses ... in the sea." They were separated from the old life in Egypt, and united to a new leader, Moses. Thus, the burial unites us in this death with the death of Christ, and the resurrection unites us in this resurrection with the resurrection of Christ (Romans 6:5). Some people believe that baptism is a necessary part of being saved. This is referred to as 'baptismal regeneration.' This is sometimes based on Mark 16:16 or Acts 2:38.

Both of these verses were written to the Jewish nation who were told to be baptized as outward evidence that they were dissociating themselves from their nation's rejection of Christ. Mark 16:16 is obviously a temporary situation during the time of the apostles, as verses 17 and 18 show.

1 Peter 3:21 – "this water symbolises baptism that now saves you also - not the removal of dirt from the body but the pledge of a good conscience towards God."

f) What follows baptism?

The pattern for believers is established in Acts 2:41,42, which is the first account of disciples being baptized after the Lord's resurrection: (1) saved then (2) baptized then (3) added to a church of God (see Session 17). Obedience in all of these steps is expected of a disciple.

REVIEW QUESTIONS

1. What are the three types of baptism referred to in the New Testament? Which ones involve water?
2. Who should be baptized in water today?
3. What does 'baptizo' mean?
4. Describe the act of baptism.
5. What is the significance of the name into which a disciple is baptized?
6. Into what name should a disciple be baptized? What does this acknowledge?
7. What is the scriptural significance of baptism?
8. What is the significance of baptism with respect to the lordship of Christ?
9. What should follow baptism?

MEMORY VERSE

Romans 6:4 – "We were therefore buried with him through baptism into death in order that, just as Christ was raised from the dead through the glory of the Father, we too may live a new life."

DISCUSSION QUESTIONS

1. Is baptism optional for a disciple? (See James 4:17)
2. What does it mean to be 'united' with Christ in His death and resurrection through baptism? (See Colossians 2:12)
3. How is Mary Magdalene an illustration of the significance of baptism in her association with Christ in Luke 8:2, John 19:25, Luke 23:55, John 20:1 and Acts 1:13,14.

ASSIGNMENT

Write a reply (with Scriptures) to someone who tells you that, since they were sprinkled as an infant, they have no further need to be baptized.

4

CONTENTS OF THE BIBLE

OBJECTIVES

1. To understand generally the subject matter and time period covered by Scripture. 2. To appreciate the reason why Scripture covers what it does and leaves out what it does.

ADVANCE READING

Read the following Scriptures and write a brief statement summarizing each: 1. Luke 24:27; 2. John 5:39; 3. Romans 15:4; 4. 2 Peter 1:19-21

TOPIC OVERVIEW

a) Introduction:

The Bible consists of 66 books; so it is really a library of books. Although it is historically and otherwise perfectly accurate, it was not written for the purpose of being a comprehensive history, book, science book, etc. It was written by God, through man, to reveal Himself, and so that men would believe on Him as a result (John 20:30,31).

b) Old Testament:

- it consists of two 'testaments' or covenants, which covered two periods of time in which God dealt with men by (a) law, and then (b) grace;
- it consists of 39 books, by many authors - and yet all perfectly consistent - and covers a lengthy period from the creation to about 400 years before the birth of Christ;
- it has several kinds of books: a) history - Genesis to Job (18 books), b) poetry - Psalms to Song of Solomon (4 books), and c) prophecies - sayings of prophets - Isaiah to Malachi (17 books);
- the application today is largely for background knowledge and to illustrate the principles in the New Testament (Romans 15:4).

c) New Testament:

- it consists of 27 books, by eight authors - Matthew, Mark, Luke (2), John (5), Paul (13), James (1), Peter (2), Judas (1), unknown (1-i.e. Hebrews) - and covers about 70 years, from the birth of Christ to about 90 A.D.;
- it has several kinds of books: a) history - Matthew to Acts (5 books), b)letters (epistles) by apostles - Romans to Jude (21 books), and c) prophecy regarding the future - Revelation (1 book);
- it is directly applicable today - it contains the gospel of salvation for sinners,and commandments of the Lord for disciples.

d) The theme:

- the overall theme of the Bible is the person and work of Christ; the Scriptures 'speak of Christ' (John 5:39) and the entire Old Testament Scriptures concerned Him (Luke 24:27); 'the Word' (John 1:1) is the subject of the written Word
- the Old Testament Scriptures contain many predictions (prophecies) about Christ; He fulfilled all of them. Here are some Old Testament verses and where they are fulfilled in the New Testament:

1. Genesis 3:15 & Galatians 4;
2. Micah 5:2 & Matthew 2:14;
3. Isaiah 7:14 & Matthew 1:18;
4. Hosea 11:1 & Matthew 2:14;
5. Isaiah 53:3 & John 1:11;
6. Zechariah 9:9 & John 12:13,14;
7. Psalm 41:9 & Matthew 26:14-16;
8. Isaiah 53:7 & Matthew 26:62,63;
9. Isaiah 53:12 & Matthew 27:38;
10. Zechariah 12:10 & John 19:34;
11. Psalm 16:10 & Matthew 28:9.

e) Example - the gospel by John:

The gospel by John presents Christ in many ways in each of its 21 chapters:

1. **The Son of God** - His deity is portrayed. "In the beginning was the Word, and the Word was with God, and the Word was God" (v.1). "We have seen his glory, the glory of the One and Only, who came from the Father, full of grace and truth" (v.14);
2. **The Son of Man** - Here we have a scene illustrating His perfect humanity. He appears as a guest at the marriage in Cana of Galilee. He mingles with men in their social activities;
3. **The Divine Teacher** - He instructs a teacher of Israel. Nicodemus says, "we know you are a teacher who has come from God" (v.2);
4. **The Soul-Winner** - He leads The Samaritan woman into the light;
5. **The Great Physician** - bending in compassion over the sufferers at the pool. He shows His divine power by the instant cure of a hopeless case (vv.8,9);
6. **The Bread of Life** - (v.48) Without Him the souls of men perish from hunger;
7. **The Water of Life** - (v.37) satisfying the thirsty heart;
8. **The Defender of the Weak** - He defends a disgraced woman (vv.3-11);

9. **The Light of the World** - (v.5). He gives light to one who was born blind (v.11);

10. **The Good Shepherd** - (v.11) - He gives His life for the sheep;

11. **The Prince of Life** - (v.25) - He calls Lazarus from the tomb (vv.43,44);

12. **The King** - He rides into Jerusalem and is acclaimed king of Israel by the crowd (vv.12-15);

13. **Servant** - He washes the disciples' feet (vv.4,5);

14. **The Comforter** - although standing under the very shadow of His cross, in utter self-forgetfulness He comforts the sorrowing disciples (v.1);

15. **The True Vine** - (v.1) He is the source of all spiritual fruit;

16. **The Giver of the Spirit** - On His departure He promised to send the other Counsellor into the world (vv.7-15);

17. **The Great Intercessor** - He offers His intercessory prayer for the disciples;

18. **The Model Sufferer** - (v.11) He submissively drinks the cup of suffering from His Father;

19. **The Uplifted Saviour** - (v.18, also 3:14). He becomes "obedient to death, even the death of the cross";

20. **The Conqueror of Death** - Four times He met and conquered "the king of terrors"; First, at the bedside of the little girl, Matthew 9:24,25; second, at the coffin of the widow's son, Luke 7:11-15; third, at the tomb of Lazarus, John 11:43,44; finally, in His own resurrection, He became a conqueror (20:11-17); Revelation 1:18);

21. **The Restorer of the Penitent** - He welcomes Peter back to the fold and commissions him to feed the sheep and lambs (vv.15-17).

REVIEW QUESTIONS

1. How many books are in the Old Testament?
2. What period of time does it cover?
3. What are the three types of books in it?
4. What is the Old Testament's application to us today?
5. How many books are in the New Testament?

6. What period of time does it cover?
7. What men wrote the New Testament books?
8. What is its application to us today?
9. What is the theme of the whole Bible?
10. What is the purpose of the Bible?
11. What are three examples of Old Testament prophecies about Christ that were fulfilled in the New Testament?

MEMORY WORK

Memorize the names of the books in the Old and New Testament.

DISCUSSION QUESTIONS

1. Which books record: [a] the delivery of Israel from Egypt [b] the songs of David and other writers [c] the activities of the apostles in the churches of God [d] the Christian's personal fellowship with God [e] the reigns of kings Saul, David and Solomon [f] the worship of the people of God today [g] future events [h] the return of exiled Jews from Babylon?
2. Who came first? Christ or Paul? Noah or Joshua? Elijah or David? Moses or Joseph?
3. What do you think is meant by John in the last verse of his gospel?
4. The ten commandments (Exodus 20:1-17) were part of the law of God given by Moses to Israel. We are no longer under that Old Testament law but rather saved by grace. Yet many of the commandments apply to us since they are explicitly restated in the New Testament. From the following Scriptures, indicate which ones do and do not apply today: (1 Corinthians 6:9; 1 Corinthians 8:6; Ephesians 4:28; Ephesians 5:3; Ephesians 6:1; 2 Timothy 2:16; 2 Timothy 3:3; 1 Peter 4:15; 1 John 5:21).
5. From your general knowledge of the Bible, what are the geographic extremities (i.e. furthest points north, south, east, west) of historical events recorded in the Bible?
6. In 2 Peter 1:19-21, Peter indicates that the written Word of God has more

authority than what they witnessed with their own eyes. Why do you think this is?

ASSIGNMENT

Write out, from memory, a list of the books of the Bible, classifying them as (a) history, (b) prophecy, (c) letter, or (d) poetry. Indicate their chronological sequence, to the extent possible.

5

THE AUTHORITY OF SCRIPTURE

OBJECTIVES

1. To understand that Scripture is complete, without error and divinely inspired. 2. To be convinced that Scripture, as revealed to us by the Holy Spirit, is totally authoritative, and thus provides entirely sufficient guidance for people today.

ADVANCE READING

Read the following Scriptures and write a brief statement of the main point of each: 1. Matthew 15:5-9; 2. Luke 4:4; 3. Deuteronomy 8:3; 4. Luke 6:46; 5. Luke 10:21-24; 6. 1 Peter 1:10-12; 7. 2 Peter 1:19-22

TOPIC OVERVIEW

"Every word of God is flawless" (Proverbs 30:5).

a) The inspiration of Scripture

This refers to the source and method by which the Bible originated. God (the Holy Spirit) was the source; men were the vehicle. They were not passive, but they were effectively controlled by the Holy Spirit:

- 2 Timothy 3:16 – "All Scripture is God-breathed";
- Jeremiah 1:9 – "I have put my words in your mouth";
- 2 Peter 1:21 – "men spoke from God as they were carried along by the Holy Spirit";

Not only were the thoughts of the writers inspired, but so were the actual words and exact grammar; for example:

- Galatians 3:16 - emphasizes the use of the singular noun;
- John 10:35 - the single word 'gods,' from a single Psalm, is referred to as Scripture which 'cannot be broken';
- Mark 12:26,27 - the tense of the verb is noted;
- Matthew 5:18 – 'jot and tittle' (RV) are small strokes used in forming or altering letters in Hebrew (like T into F in English).

Thus we believe in:

- **verbal** inspiration - the words are inspired, not just the thoughts;
- **plenary** inspiration - all words are inspired, even obscure parts;
- **infallible** inspiration - Scripture is reliable and does not mislead;
- **inerrant** inspiration - it is true and error-free in all its parts;

Inspiration refers to the original writings. It is possible that copies and translations may contain textual errors. However: Jeremiah 1:12 - God watches over His Word.'

'Textual criticism' - scholars have carefully compared the present texts to the originals; these have proved to be virtually identical, except for a few disputed passages (none of which affects key doctrines). Any errors that may exist in the present text are due to human error in copying. The original text, as it came from God, was error-free or else it could not be relied on for such truths as our salvation.

b) The canon of Scripture

This term refers to the collection of books which were considered by religious scholars as being of divine origin, which is why they are in our Bible. 'Canon' means 'measuring stick' in Greek. The primary criterion for considering Old Testament Scriptures to be in the canon was that they were affirmed by the Lord Jesus. For example:

- Luke 24:27 - Christ, after His resurrection, on the way to Emmaus;
- Luke 11:51 - He referred to the murders of Abel (Genesis 4) and Zechariah (2 Chronicles 24); these were the first and last historical books in the Jewish Old Testament.

Criteria for considering New Testament books as part of the canon were:

- they were the work of an apostle or close associate;
- the text must be approved by the majority of the churches as genuine;
- it must conform to the rest of the revealed doctrine.

While the apostles lived, they were the authority and there was no need for the canon. Their words and writings were circulated widely among believers (e.g. 1 Timothy 1:15; 2 Peter 3:15,16). After their death, it was necessary to agree on the canon to counteract erroneous doctrine, which had been predicted (Acts 20:29,30). The canon was first established by A.D. 367.

The Apocrypha is a collection of 7 to 16 books which appeared between the Old and New Testaments. Examples are: 1 & 2 Esdras, Tobit, Judith, Song of the Three Holy Children, 1 & 2 Maccabees. Over the years, ecclesiastical opinion has varied about whether they were canonical. Eleven of them appear in modern Catholic versions of the Bible. However they are excluded from most Protestant versions because they were never referred to by Christ (or the apostles) and they are generally inferior to the books in Scripture.

c) Versions of Scripture

There were 3 major copies of the original manuscripts:

- Codex Sinaiticus (Greek Bible) - 4th century. Now in the British Museum;
- Codex Alexandrinus (Greek Bible) - 5th century. Also in the British Museum;
- Codex Vaticanus (whole Bible) - 4th century. In the Vatican Library in Rome.

Ancient Versions:

- Septuagint (A.D. 250) - translation of Hebrew Old Testament into Greek for Alexander the Great;
- Vulgate (A.D. 400) - translation of entire Bible into Latin. Was the standard Catholic Bible for 1000 years;
- Masoretic Text (A.D. 500-950) - authoritative version of the Old Testament by Jewish scholars; first introduced vowels into the Hebrew text;

Early English Versions:

After the Dark Ages, English language translations were produced by Wycliffe (1380), Tyndale (1525), Coverdale (1535), and Matthew (1537), largely from the Latin. Others were the Great Bible (1539) and the Geneva Bible (1560). The most significant were:

- Douay Bible (1610) – a Roman Catholic version from the Latin Vulgate;
- King James (Authorized) (1611) – from the original languages; authorized by King James I; the most popular version;
- Revised Version (1885) – a more exact translation, from the most ancient copies. Available in English and American versions. Is generally the best study Bible;
- American Standard Version (1901) – American revisions to the Revised Version.

More recent English Versions:

- Revised Standard Version (1952) – revisions to the American Standard. Revised again in 1971 as the New American Standard Bible (NASB);
- Amplified Bible (1965);
- Jerusalem Bible (1966) – Roman Catholic; originally in French;
- New English Bible (1970);
- Living Bible (1971) – is a paraphrase, not a translation;
- New International Version (1978, 2011) – translated the meaning of whole sentences, rather than just individual words; thus involved a greater degree of interpretation;
- New King James Version (1982) – the original KJV with modern grammar;
- English Standard Version (2001).

Hebrew and Greek are precise languages, with different words being used to convey shades of meaning. These distinctions are sometimes lost in the English translation. Help in understanding these distinctions can be obtained from a concordance, a lexicon or an English dictionary of Hebrew and Greek words.The versions which have been approved for public use in the Churches of God, based on thorough analysis, are: RV, KJV, NIV, NASB, NKJV, ESV. Use of other versions has been avoided since some versions are less accurate, and great variety of versions can cause confusion to the audience.

d) The implications of the authority of Scripture

"Show me what is in that book, and you put me under an obligation to submit to it" (John Drain, 1986, in an address). Because the Bible is inspired, it is error-free ... thus it is totally reliable ... and sufficient (needing nothing to supplement it) ... and is authoritative over our lives.

- It is the basis of our revelation about our salvation (Romans 10:17);
- It is the rule for Christians' way of life (Romans 15:4);
- It is the standard by which all men shall be judged (John 12:48);
- It is its own interpreter (Acts 17:11);
- It is used by the Holy Spirit for our sanctification (John 17:17);
- It is worthy of memorization (Psalm 119:11);
- It is to be taught to others (Deuteronomy 6:6-9).

REVIEW QUESTIONS

1. In what sense is Scripture inspired?
2. In what languages were the original Scriptures written?
3. What is meant by the term 'the canon of Scripture'?
4. Why don't we need to possess the actual original manuscripts today in order to be sure our Bible is divinely inspired?
5. Which versions are most reliable for study purposes?
6. What is the difference between a translation and a transliteration?
7. Which English language versions have been subsequently updated?
8. What did John Drain mean by his statement?

MEMORY VERSE

2 Timothy 3:16,17 - "All Scripture is God-breathed and is useful for teaching, rebuking, correcting and training in righteousness, so that the man of God may be thoroughly equipped for every good work."

DISCUSSION QUESTIONS

1. How can we explain apparent differences in accounts given by various Bible writers of the same event? (e.g. Matthew 20:30 vs. Mark 10:46; 1 Corinthians 10:8 vs. Numbers 25:9)
2. How do we know that the canon of Scripture is complete, and that God is not inspiring fresh Scripture today?
3. What is the difference between taking the Bible 'literally' and saying we believe it is 'true'?
4. What are the major risks if Christians give up believing in the divine inspiration and inerrancy of Scripture?

ASSIGNMENT

List what problems you foresee if we were to hold that the Bible was generally correct but was not inerrant on matters of science, history, or genealogies.

6

BIBLE READING AND STUDY

OBJECTIVES

1. To realize the importance of regular reading and study of the Scriptures. 2. To understand how to get the most out of Bible reading and study.

ADVANCE READING

Read the following Scriptures and write a brief statement summarizing the main point of each: 1. Joshua 1:8; 2. Job 23:12; 3. Psalm 119:9-11; 4. Luke 24:27; 5. Acts 17:11; 6. 2 Timothy 2:15

TOPIC OVERVIEW

a) Why study the Bible?

It should be considered a 'must,' not an option. Our views are no substitute. Jesus often condemned religious people for their lack of knowledge and application of Scripture (e.g. Matthew 12:3,4; 19:4; 21:42). The purpose of Bible study is correctly to understand its meaning, and then to do it. The results of this will be:

- cleansing (sanctification) of our lives (Psalm 119:9; Ephesians 5:26);
- Bible study shows us more of God's righteousness and our sinfulness which encourages us to confess our sins and then live according to God's direction (1 John 1:6-10);
- spiritual growth and maturity; the teaching of Scripture is referred to as milk and meat (Hebrews 5:12);
- defence against Satan's temptations (Ephesians 6:10,17), including wrong doctrine
- greater knowledge of Christ, who is also called the 'Word' (John 1:1).

b) How to study the Bible

- **Reading** - use an accurate version (e.g. Revised Version)- read very attentively - make notes- don't substitute commentaries for the actual reading of Scripture;
- **Analyzing** - compare one Scripture with another- use a concordance or margin references to find the comparable Scriptures- use commentaries to supplement this analysis;
- **Meditating** - think about the Scriptures - pray to know the real meaning, since it can only be known by the Holy Spirit revealing it to you - imitate the Lord Jesus in this respect (Psalm 1:1);
- **Applying** - the benefit will be lost unless you carry out what you have learned (Matthew 7:24)- as a disciple, you have already committed to do the Lord's will; your study helps you to know what to do.

c) Things to look for

You can study a book of the Bible, chapter by chapter. Or you can study a particular subject; examples are: titles of Christ; key words (e.g. redemption, resurrection, church).

- look for explicit commands of the Lord that apply today;
- look for promises that apply to us;

- look for things (people, events, objects) that present a picture of Christ;
- look for general principles that apply today.

d) Interpreting the Scriptures

The meaning of Scripture is not always obvious. A lot of symbolism is used. There are some general principles for interpreting correctly:

- the most direct and obvious meaning of a Scripture is usually the correct one; (for example, the word 'flesh' has a different meaning in John 6:53 from Galatians 5:17 (RV), as is clear from the context);
- interpret a Scripture in a way which is consistent with other Scriptures ("no prophecy of Scripture came about by the prophet's own interpretation" – 2 Peter 1:20);
- the first occurrence of a truth in Scripture often gives a strong clue to its meaning; which is why Genesis is called the 'seedplot of the Bible';
- a common form of symbolism is types; a 'type' is something or someone in the Old Testament which, every time it is mentioned symbolizes the 'antitype' - i.e. a truth (often relating to Christ) in the New Testament. An example of a 'type' is the blood of animal sacrifices, which are a type of Christ's atoning blood;
- an evil thing cannot be a type of a good thing;
- the antitype must be greater than the type (e.g. the tabernacle as a type of the heavenly sanctuary);
- don't read everything that is in the antitype into the type - this is 'spiritualizing';
- another form of symbolism is parables; similar principles of interpretation apply as to types.

e) Aids to use in Bible study

- **Concordance** - to find other occurrences of the same word. The simplest to use is 'Young's; a more advanced one is 'Strong's'. Use a complete concordance, rather than an abridged edition. Note what version of the Bible it uses;
- **Bible Dictionary** - to define and explain Bible words and names, because their original meaning was not always its meaning today, and some words are used with several meanings (e.g. 'field' refers to the world in Matthew 13:24 but to the church of God in 1 Corinthians 3:9 NIV);
- **Churches of God Literature** - e.g. Needed Truth and Bible Studies. Annual volumes are available and there are indexes of articles and subjects covered. John Miller's Commentary on the Epistles and many other books and booklets are obtainable via Hayes Press and/or your overseers;
- **Commentaries** - these can be useful but they should not be relied on too much, especially before you have done your own study. They are not generally a reliable source on doctrine. For example, they often fail to distinguish 'the Church the Body of Christ' from 'the church of God.' Ask an overseer for advice before buying one as they are too expensive to make a bad choice;
- **Margin and Chain References in your Bible** - these can direct you to other related Scriptures. As with commentaries, use them with care;
- **Bible Atlas** - to understand the significance of the geography.

f) Some practical advice

1. plan enough time to study;
2. use a place which has no distractions;
3. before you start, pray for understanding and concentration;
4. make notes of key points;
5. give enough time to meditate and think over what you have studied;
6. use study aids (see above);
7. ask for help on questions that arise; but be careful who you ask (Jesus

warned about 'blind guides' in Matthew 15:14); overseers have a desire and a responsibility to help.

REVIEW QUESTIONS

1. Give three reasons to show why Bible study is a necessity.
2. What is the difference between the Bible and other books?
3. What is meditation?
4. What are 'types' and 'antitypes'?
5. What things can you look for during Bible study?
6. What is 'spiritualizing'?
7. What Bible study aids require caution in their use?

MEMORY VERSE

2 Timothy 2:15 - "Do your best to present yourself to God as one approved, a worker who does not need to be ashamed and who correctly handles the word of truth."

DISCUSSION QUESTIONS

1. How will I know if I'm not devoting enough time to Bible study?
2. What are the main dangers to avoid when studying the Bible?
3. What are the differences between study of the Bible and other study?
4. What are the requirements for a good group Bible Study?

ASSIGNMENT

Using the methods described in this session, complete a written study on the word 'bless.' Include: the commands of the Lord in this regard; prerequisites to His blessing people; and personal application.

7

PRAYER

OBJECTIVES

1. To understand the conditions which are necessary for successful prayer. 2. To develop the habit of frequent, fervent prayer.

ADVANCE READING

Read the following Scriptures and write a brief statement summarizing each: 1. John 16:24; 2. Acts 12:5; 3. Romans 8:26,27; 4. 1 Thessalonians 5:17; 5. James 4:3; 6. James 5:16

TOPIC OVERVIEW

a) Prayer - a privilege and a necessity

- prayer is both a privilege of being a child of God and a necessity to continue to grow spiritually;
- prayer (in a narrow sense) is making requests to God as our Father;
- prayer (in a wider sense) includes all communication to God (worship, praise, confession, thanksgiving, etc.).

God delights to hear our prayers and to answer them. Together with meditating on what we read in the Bible, it is how we 'commune' with God (Isaiah 40:31).

b) Conditions of answered prayer

God has promised in Scripture to answer our prayer if:

- we ask according to His will (1 John 5:14);
- we ask in faith (Matthew 21:22);
- we don't ask selfishly (James 4:3);
- we ask in the name (authority) of the Lord Jesus Christ (John 16:24).

c) The communications channel

All three Persons of the Godhead are involved when we pray (Ephesians 2:18):

- **to** the Father, who is the giver (the source) (James 1:17);
- **through** Christ, who intercedes with God the Father in heaven (Hebrews 7:25) on the basis of His finished work of reconciling us to God;
- **in** the Spirit, who intercedes within us, communicating with our human spirit, which is what we pray with (Romans 8:26,27).

d) Examples of praying people

Some examples of men of prayer are: Christ (Mark 1:35; Luke 22:41,42; John 17:1); Daniel (Daniel 6:10); Elijah (James 5:17,18). Examples of women of prayer include: Hannah (1 Samuel 1:10) and Anna (Luke 2:36,37).

Matthew 6:9-13 is called 'the Lord's prayer'; actually it is 'the disciples' prayer'. The Lord's own prayer is in John 17. Christ taught His disciples to pray first for God's kingdom and will, before asking for themselves. He taught them not to use vain repetitions. People in Scripture who prayed had regular times to pray each day, and also prayed spontaneously. We are to pray frequently (1 Thessalonians 5:17).

e) Types of prayer (see 1 Timothy 2:1)

- **supplication** - pleading (e.g. Luke 11:5-13 - loaves of bread);
- **intercession** - for others (e.g. Genesis 18:23-33 - Abraham interceding for Lot);
- **thanksgiving** - for God's goodness (Psalm 92:1; Philippians 4:6);
- **confession** - for sin (1 John 1:9); unconfessed sin is a barrier to fellowship with God and to answered prayer (1 John 1:6,7; Psalm 66:18).

f) Physical posture in prayer

Our posture in prayer (standing, sitting, kneeling) is not important, other than to show reverence. Closing our eyes is simply to help us concentrate.

g) Collective prayer

In addition to individual prayer, churches of God are to meet for 'the prayers'- times of collective prayer (Acts 2:42; Hebrews 4:16) - an example of this was the prayer meeting of the Church of God in Jerusalem in Acts 12. The house of God is to be a place of prayer for all people (Mark 11:17); the men are to lead the Assembly in prayer (1 Timothy 2:8), while the women are to keep their hair covered (1 Corinthians 11:5) as a sign of the leadership of the men. All should say 'Amen' to indicate it is a united prayer (1 Corinthians 14:16) - a symbol of this was the incense that burned in the golden altar in the tabernacle and temple (Exodus 30:1; Luke 1:10; Revelation 8:3).

h) Addressing God in prayer

In prayer, God may be addressed as 'God', as 'Father', or as 'God our Father.' His highest title in worship is "the God and Father of the Lord Jesus Christ" (Ephesians 1:3).

REVIEW QUESTIONS

1. Who can pray to God as their Father?
2. Who do you pray to?
3. In whose name do we pray?
4. What is the difference between prayer and the prayers?
5. What is supplication?
6. What is thanksgiving?
7. What is confession?
8. What are the conditions for answered prayer?

MEMORY VERSE

1 John 5:14 - "This is the confidence we have in approaching God: that if we ask anything according to his will, he hears us."

DISCUSSION QUESTIONS

1. Does God answer the prayer of unbelievers?
2. What is the result of your not confessing your sin to God?
3. What did Jesus mean in Matthew 26:41: 'watch and pray'?
4. What is fasting, and what is it for (e.g. Acts 13:3)?
5. Where is the best place to pray?
6. What is the lesson from Moses' prayer in Exodus 17:8-13?
7. What are things for which my Assembly should be praying?
8. Name one prayer that you have had answered recently?
9. How much time do you regularly spend in prayer?

10. Is the length of the prayer important?

ASSIGNMENT

Make a list of seven people or things that you are concerned about, that you believe are within God's will. Each day this week, pray earnestly in private for one of them.

8

CHRISTLIKENESS

OBJECTIVES

1. To understand the pleasure God gets from disciples becoming more like His Son, in whom He delights. 2. To appreciate the attributes of Christ and how to obtain them.

ADVANCE READING

Read the following Scriptures and write a brief statement summarizing each one: 1. Matthew 11:29; 2. John 13:15; 3. 1 Corinthians 11:1; 4. Galatians 4:19; 5. Philippians 2:5-11; 6. Philippians 3:21; 7. Hebrews 3:1; 8. Hebrews 12:2; 9. 1 Peter 2:21

TOPIC OVERVIEW

a) The goal:

The goal of mankind, in the mind of God our Creator, is not self-improvement or reformation, but to become as close as possible to Christ ("attaining to the whole measure of the fulness of Christ" - Ephesians 4:13). Christ is God's 'well-beloved' Son; God the Father delights in Christ (Matthew 12:18). Paul longed (with an intensity like childbirth) "until Christ is formed in you" (Galatians 4:19).

b) The reason:

It should be the outgrowth of our love and gratitude to Christ for our salvation (1 John 4:19). The more we know Him, the more we will admire Him and want to emulate Him (2 Peter 3:18). It is the greatest way of bringing pleasure to God in our lives (Romans 14:18).

c) What does it mean to be 'like Christ'?

It does not mean: a) to be like Him in appearance, b) to be sinless, or c) to be equal with Him as God. It does mean: to have the same attitude, and as a result to have the same behaviour as He had during His life.

d) What was Christ like in His life on earth?

- He was totally un-self-centered;
- He had no personal ambition; He was devoted to pleasing God;
- He was humble; He served others;
- He was totally submissive to the Word of God;
- He was constantly alert to God speaking to Him and to the Scriptures;
- He was totally holy in "all manner of living" (1 Peter 1:15 RV) because of His association with a holy God;
- He "loved righteousness and hated iniquity" - these are strong words;
- He was totally loving in His relationships with others e.g. 2 Corinthians 10:1 RV – "the meekness and gentleness of Christ."

e) The process:

We are not naturally like Christ, nor do we naturally want to be. It is impossible to become Christ-like just with our own efforts; we will constantly be frustrated; it is something we must let the Holy Spirit do in us. It is not a single event, or a series of events, it is a never-ending progressive process. Scripture describes it as "putting on Christ" - a positive action (Romans 13:14 - like putting on clothes). It involves:

- **learning about Christ** (Matthew 11:29; Philippians 3:10) - from the Scriptures, which speak of Him (especially the life of Christ as recorded in the gospels);
- **imitating His conduct** (1 Corinthians 11:1) - e.g. "compassion, kindness, humility, gentleness and patience, forgiveness in love" (Colossians 3:12-15);
- **abiding in Him** (John 15:1-8 RV) so that we may be fruitful, as He was - i.e. spend time communing with Him;
- **obeying Christ's commands** (2 John vv.4-6).

f) The culmination:

At the Rapture, we shall not only be "with Christ," we shall be "like Him." We will have bodies "like his glorious body" (Philippians 3:21) (this is referred to as "the redemption of our bodies" - Romans 8:23); our bodies will be immortal. Our mind and attitude will also be like His. If we humble ourselves now, God will exalt us then, as He did Christ (Philippians 2:9).

REVIEW QUESTIONS

1. What did Paul mean 'until Christ be formed in you', and why was it important?
2. Why should a disciple want to be like Christ? Give two or three reasons.
3. What does it mean, and what does it not mean, to be 'like Christ'?

4. Describe briefly what Christ was like as a Man on earth.

5. Describe the scriptural process for becoming like Christ.

6. In what way will Christians become Christlike at the rapture?

MEMORY VERSE

Philippians 2:5-8 (RV) - "Have this mind in you, which was also in Christ Jesus: who, being in the form of God, counted it not a prize to be on an equality with God, but emptied himself, taking the form of a servant, being made in the likeness of men; and being found in fashion as a man, he humbled himself, becoming obedient even unto death, yea, the death of the cross."

DISCUSSION QUESTIONS

1. It was the apostle Paul's aim to imitate Christ. Show how Paul was different as a result of this, compared with before his salvation (e.g. Philippians 1:21).

2. Explain Matthew 10:24,25 (also Luke 6:40).

3. What are your biggest hindrances to becoming increasingly Christlike? Is it a realistic objective today?

4. Precisely what can the Bible do in helping us to actually become more like Christ?

5. Identify three practical ways in which you can "put on Christ."

ASSIGNMENT

Select any three chapters in the gospels and identify references to the attitude or behaviour of Christ in particular situations. For each one, indicate a similar situation which you encounter and what your natural reaction is. Compare your reaction with Christ's.

9

VICTORY OVER SIN

OBJECTIVES

1. To understand that, although we have been saved from the penalty of sin, we still have a strong tendency to sin. 2. To realize how vital it is to have victory over sin in our lives, and how to achieve it.

ADVANCE READING

Read the following Scriptures and write a statement summarizing each one: 1. Romans 6:1-14; 2. James 1:13-15; 3. 1 John 1:8-2:2; 4. Hebrews 12:1

TOPIC OVERVIEW

a) Our initial sinful condition:

Every human being (except Christ, Adam and Eve) was 'born in sins' (John 9:34 RV). David described it as being 'shapen in iniquity' (Psalm 51:5 RV). We all have a sinful nature, that causes us to commit sins. In our natural condition, we are 'dead through our trespasses and sins' (Ephesians 2:1 RV). Only God can forgive sins. But in order to forgive, without compromising His standards of righteousness, the penalty must be paid by a sinless human being. It was for this reason that Christ became human, lived a sinless life (uniquely) and died on Calvary as a sin offering for the rest of mankind. He won victory over all sin for all time. In anticipation of this, in the Old Testament, animal sacrifices were accepted by God as symbolic sin offerings. Because Christ's sacrifice was perfect, there is no need for any further sin offering.

b) The result of salvation:

At the point of an individual's salvation through faith, that person is born again, made alive unto God and justified (made righteous in God's sight). Just as the disobedience of Adam has made all of us sinners by inheritance, so the obedience of Christ makes all who accept that sacrifice righteous, never to die again spiritually. Our justification before God, and our forgiveness by Him, is permanent and unconditional (Romans 8:1).

c) Our continuing sinful nature:

Despite our salvation, we still keep our sinful nature ('the flesh'), which creates a conflict with the new nature, since we still have the tendency to sin. Sin in the life of a Christian causes a severance in his fellowship with God and a lack of effectiveness in service (1 John 1). It can inhibit prayer (e.g. Psalm 66:18). It can bring about the judgment of God (e.g. 1 Corinthians 11:27-32).

Sin can be accidental (through ignorance and weakness), or much more seriously, deliberate (through rebellion and stubbornness). There are degrees of seriousness of sin (from simple mistakes) to extreme moral sins (like murder and fornication). We are not always aware we have sinned, especially if our consciences are dulled through repetitive sin. Sins can be committed by individuals (e.g. Ananias and Sapphira who lied to God - Acts 5:4 - the consequence was death). They can also be committed by the people of God (e.g. Achan – 'Israel has sinned' - Joshua 7:11 - consequence was defeat).

d) The seriousness of sin:

God regards all sin as serious because of His holy nature. It is a violation of His standard of righteousness. Sin that is not dealt with can spread to others and dull our conscience to further sin.

e) Temptation:

Sin is often the outgrowth of temptation. Temptation usually comes from outside - what we see, hear, etc. - often prompted by Satan (James 1:12-15). We are told to "Resist the devil, and he will flee from you" (James 4:7). Even Christ was tempted (Luke 4:1-13), but it didn't result in sin. When Christ was tempted by Satan, He resisted him by quoting the Word of God, not by divine means, showing us that we can do the same. Temptation, however, is not the same as sin (James 1:13-15). God will not let us be tempted more than we can take (1 Corinthians 10:13).

f) Dealing with sin:

Even as believers, if we think we don't sin and have reached 'sinless perfection', we are wrong (1 John 1:8). The Holy Spirit convicts of sin (John 16:8) to bring it to our memory to help us to confess it. This is aided by reading Scripture regularly. What we are to do, as soon as we become conscious of sin, is to stop it and to confess that sin to God (1 John 1:9) - that is, tell Him in prayer and acknowledge that it is wrong.

If we do confess our sins, every time He will (1) forgive us, and (2) cleanse us - because of His own faithfulness, no matter how serious the sin. There may also be the consequences of the sin (e.g. damage to another person) to be dealt with. Because of the negative effects of sin in the disciple's life, he should keep 'short accounts' with God - that is, not let sin go unconfessed for very long. If our sin is against another person, we then should also confess it to them (James 5:16). An example of this is the prodigal son in Luke 15 who finally realized he had sinned and so he decided to go back home and say "Father, I have sinned against heaven and against you" (note the sequence).

g) Practical ways to prevent sin:

- Know your weaknesses (e.g. jealousy, anger, gossip, partiality, pride, taking offence, disobedience, neglect, judging others, blaming others ...?);
- Don't go 'as far as you can' - avoid even the appearance of evil (1 Thessalonians 5:22);
- Keep in close communion with the Lord (by prayer and Bible reading), and self-examination; by acting on your conscience, it becomes stronger, and your judgment about what is good and bad gets better (Hebrews 5:14);
- Realize that it's your flesh that's being appealed to in temptation; put on the whole armour of God (Ephesians 6:13-18) so we have the opportunity of moving from being dead in sins (Ephesians 2:1) to being dead to sin (Romans 6:2).

REVIEW QUESTIONS

1. What is mankind's inherited nature, without exception?
2. What is the difference between temptation and sin?
3. How can God righteously avoid punishing Christians who sin?
4. What should we do as soon as we become conscious that we have sinned?
5. What is the effect of not doing that?
6. What is meant by "dead in sins" (Ephesians 2:1) and "dead to sin" (Romans 6:11)?
7. What is meant when it says that Christ a) knew no sin (2 Corinthians 5:21 RV)? b) did no sin (1 Peter 2:22) and c) in Him was no sin (1 John 3:5)?
8. What has God promised to do if we confess our sin (1 John 1:9)?

MEMORY VERSE

1 John 1:9 - "If we confess our sins, he is faithful and just and will forgive us our sins and purify us from all unrighteousness."

DISCUSSION QUESTIONS

1. In what ways does Scripture describe our inherited sinful nature (Ephesians 2:1-3; Romans 3:9-18)?
2. Explain what is meant by Romans 5:19.
3. What are some types of (a) unintentional sins and (b) intentional sins that you are susceptible to?
4. When we sin after we become a born again believer, does it affect our salvation?
5. What should you do if you are aware that another disciple has committed a serious sin?
6. What effect do you think unconfessed sin over a long period of time has?
7. What does it mean that Christ was made 'to be sin'? (2 Corinthians 5:21)
8. Explain Romans 6:13.

ASSIGNMENT

During this week, stop at the end of each day and try to recall any times that you sinned and did not confess it to God. If there were any, confess it then.

10

FAMILY LIFE

OBJECTIVES

1. To understand the importance of a proper family life in God's arrangement for His disciples. 2. To understand the roles and responsibilities of each person in a family.

ADVANCE READING

Read the following Scriptures and write a brief statement summarizing each one: 1. Psalm 68:6; 2. Ephesians 5:22-33; 3. 1 Corinthians 7:1-39; 4. Ephesians 6:1-4; 5. Genesis 2:22-24; 6. 1 Timothy 4:12; 7. Luke 2:41-52

TOPIC OVERVIEW

a) Our spiritual family:

By the new birth we become children of God (John 1:12,13; 1 John 3:1) - we can never lose our place in His family. God is our Father - we can pray 'Our Father' - by 'adoption' He puts us in the position of a son and heir; this is like a Jewish boy who, before the age of 12, has not any special status in the household. After his Bar-mitzvah at age 12, he is put in the position of a son and an heir of his father (Galatians 4:1-7).

Being a 'son' of God involves obedience - being led by the Spirit of God (Romans 8:14-17). It brings about God's fatherly discipline (Hebrews 12:7) and it involves separation from things that are not of God (2 Corinthians 6:14-18). Marriage is an illustration of the union between Christ and the Church which is His Body (Ephesians 5:31,32; Genesis 2:22-24). His 'marriage' will never suffer from separation or divorce. Family life is central to God's plan for human life.

b) Husbands and wives:

Husbands are to love their wives as much as themselves (Ephesians 5:28). They are the head of the wife, as Christ is their head (1 Corinthians 11:3) and should exercise loving leadership in the marriage. They are to be gentle to their wives (Colossians 3:19), loving them (Ephesians 5:25) and being considerate to them (1 Peter 3:7). Wives are to submit to the leadership of their husbands as unto the Lord (Ephesians 5:22). They should learn from their husbands (1 Corinthians 14:35). They should not leave their husbands (1 Corinthians 7:10).

Those 'in the Lord' (i.e. in the house of God) should only be married to someone 'in the Lord' (1 Corinthians 7:39). The man and woman are not independent in the Lord (1 Corinthians 11:11). Marriage should be permanent - until death, as is also the case legally (Romans 7:2). God joins the husband and wife and no one should put them apart (Mark 10:9). God hates divorce (Malachi 2:16) - divorce, and remarriage after divorce, are wrong and require putting away from a church of God; however they can be repented of, permitting reception or restoration to the Fellowship. Marital separation is to be avoided and everything possible done to achieve a reconciliation (1 Corinthians 7:10,11).

A couple are to be faithful to each other sexually, and to honour their marriage vows (Hebrews 13:4) - adultery is a moral sin. A husband and wife should not deprive each other sexually (1 Corinthians 7:3-5).

c) Parents:

It is the responsibility of fathers to rule the household (1 Timothy 3:4) and of mothers to bring up children (1 Timothy 5:10,14) - parenting is thus a joint responsibility. In the case of a single parent household, it is very difficult to do this alone. Children are a heritage from the Lord (Psalm 127:3). Parents are to bring them up in the nurture and discipline of the Lord (Ephesians 6:4). Fathers are instructed to do the following with respect to their children:

- instruct and train them (Ephesians 6:4);
- answer their questions (Joshua 4:21,22);
- discipline them (Hebrews 12:10) - Eli was condemned by God for failing to restrain his sinful sons (1 Samuel 3:13);
- not set out to provoke them (Ephesians 6:4 RV);
- set standards for them by word and example, to create a godly home environment.

This may include, for example:

- acceptable language;
- use of time for Bible study and prayer;
- showing love and respect to family members and others;
- showing diligence in the Lord's things;
- regular attendance at assembly gatherings;
- putting separation into effect, by encouraging and discouraging particular activities, including entertainment and friendship;
- dealing with disagreements;
- showing hospitality;
- exercising care in the use of television, radio, videos, magazines, etc.;
- demonstrating proper priorities regarding earning money, and spending

money.

Mothers are to care for their children (Titus 2:4) and to instruct them (2 Timothy 1:5). They must run the household on a day-to-day basis; examples:

- planning chores around spiritual activities, not instead of them (Luke 10:38-42);
- allowing time to introduce young children to the Scriptures;
- avoiding a 'rush to the meeting' ritual;
- showing modesty in dress and actions (1 Timothy 2:9);
- supporting the father's disciplinary measures.

d) Children:

Children should obey their parents, and be respectful and submissive to them (Ephesians 6:1). Even when they are adults themselves, they should continue to honour their parents (Ephesians 6:2). God hates rebellion as much as witchcraft (1 Samuel 15:23 RV). Christian children should therefore not necessarily expect to be treated as a non-Christian child would. Even Jesus as a child was subject to His parents (Luke 2:51). If a young disciple is living at home with non-Christian parents, they may expect him or her to do things contrary to Scripture.

The child must continue to respect them as parents but there may be occasional instances where there may be a need to assess the claims of Christ (Acts 5:29) since obedience to parents is 'in the Lord' (Ephesians 6:1). Children should ask for advice from godly adults before doing this. Scripture does not give special guidance for teens since the same scriptural injunctions apply. 'Youth' is a time of potential and opportunity (1 Timothy 4:12; 1 John 2:13,14). Teens and older ones still living with parents have to recognize that, despite their age, they are still under the 'house rules' of the head of the house. When children become older, they have an obligation to provide for their parents if necessary (1 Timothy 5:8).

e) Christian homes:

Christian homes should be distinguished by their peaceful and spiritual tone. Example: the home of Martha, Lazarus and Mary in Bethany (Luke 10:38; John 11:20; John 12:2). Talking about the Scriptures should be a frequent and natural activity (Deuteronomy 6:6-9). Christian homes provide an opportunity to include others who do not have that advantage Christian homes also provide a place for outreach and Bible study for others (Acts 18:26).

REVIEW QUESTIONS

1. What do fathers have to avoid when making demands of their children?
2. What is the spiritual truth typified by marriage?
3. Who did God condemn for failing to restrain his sinful sons?
4. Who is supposed to rule the household?
5. What is necessary to accomplish regular devotional times as a family?
6. What is the difference between 'children of God' and 'sons of God'?
7. What is the primary responsibility of husbands and wives to each other?
8. What does it mean to be married 'in the Lord'?
9. What is God's attitude to divorce and separation?
10. How serious is adultery?
11. What are fathers' and mothers' responsibilities to their children?
12. What is the responsibility of children to their parents?
13. What are desirable characteristics of a Christian home?

MEMORY VERSE

Genesis 18:19 - "For I have chosen him, so that he will direct his children and his household after him to keep the way of the Lord by doing what is right and just, so that the Lord will bring about for Abraham what he has promised him."

DISCUSSION QUESTIONS

1. Aquila and Priscilla are a New Testament example of a godly couple. Refer to Acts 18:2,26; Romans 16:3-5; 2 Timothy 4:19. Discuss how they served the Lord and what lessons there are for a husband and wife today.
2. Give some examples of how fathers could incorrectly provoke their children.
3. What are the major difficulties in having a regular devotional time as a family, and how can they be overcome?
4. To what extent should parents dictate a family dress code?
5. What is the difference between subjection (which is expected of wives and children) and inferiority?
6. When is it acceptable for children to disobey their parents?
7. How could your family life be improved?

ASSIGNMENT

Make a list of the ways in which the testimony of the churches of God will be adversely affected if there is a lowering of standards in the family lives of the saints.

11

MAKING OTHER DISCIPLES

OBJECTIVES

1. To understand the importance in God's plans that disciples should be the means of making other disciples. 2. To learn practical ways of being effective in making other disciples.

ADVANCE READING

Read the following Scriptures and write a brief statement summarizing each one: 1. Matthew 28:19; 2. Acts 17:16-34; 3. Proverbs 11:30; 4. 1 Timothy 2:4; 5. 1 Peter 2:12

TOPIC OVERVIEW

a) Why should we make other disciples?

It is the means God has chosen; rather than direct divine communicating, He chooses to use human instruments (although the power comes from the Holy Spirit). The apostle Paul said: "God ... was pleased to reveal his Son in me so that I might preach him ..." (Galatians 1:15,16). It was a direct command from

Christ to His apostles – "go and make disciples" (Matthew 28:19). Making other disciples has a very valuable effect on the disciples who do it, and it provides an outlet which all disciples can have for their service to God.

b) How are disciples made?

Disciples are not born, they are made - by other disciples. It is an on-going process which involves winning them for Christ, and instructing and helping them. The goal is not just that they should be saved eternally, but that they should also become obedient followers of the Lord Jesus in their lives, in a church of God. It involves:

- **witnessing** (Acts 23:11) - sharing your own faith and experience;
- **testifying** (Acts 20:21) - talking about Christ;
- **soul-winning** (Proverbs 11:30) - urging them to give themselves to Christ;
- **instructing** (2 Timothy 2:25) - explaining Scripture, and correcting wrong ideas.

At some early stage, a disciple should be baptized in water, and then systematically taught (Matthew 28:19,20; Acts 18:8).

c) Who should do it?

Some have been given the spiritual gift of evangelism (Ephesians 4:11). But making disciples is not restricted to evangelists and full-time Lord's Servants, or even to more experienced Christians, but is for all disciples to the extent they are able:

- "as much as in me is, I am ready to preach the gospel" (Romans 1:15 RV);
- "what I received I passed on to you" (1 Corinthians 15:3);
- "do it with the strength God provides, so that in all things God may be praised through Jesus Christ" (1 Peter 4:11).

It should be done both by individuals and by the churches of God collectively (e.g. 1 Thessalonians 1:8).

d) Of whom should we make disciples?

- Everyone who is not already a committed, obedient disciple – "God wants all men to be saved and to come to a knowledge of the truth" (1 Timothy 2:4). Jesus said, "Come, follow me and I will make you fishers of men" (Mark 1:17) – that is, to 'catch' them alive. The devil has already caught them alive (same Greek word) in a trap – see 2 Timothy 2:26. We can both take advantage of opportunities as they arise (1 Peter 3:15) and also set out deliberately to win them. We can direct our efforts to friends, relatives and acquaintances, taking advantage of our existing relationship with them whereby they are more likely to trust us (e.g. John 1:41; 4:28-30). We can also make contact with strangers (e.g. John 4), through such means as: 'chance' meetings, 'cold calls' at their homes, distributing leaflets and other literature, invitations to assembly meetings, radio addresses, social media, websites and open air preaching.

e) How to go about it:

Following is a suggested sequence of steps, for practical guidance, to be adapted to individual circumstances:

[1] **Live as a disciple** - people notice your lifestyle; what you say should be consistent with what you do; your manner of life will draw some. (e.g. your language, using your Bible, praying, your behaviour to others, how you spend your free time, your concern for others, your topics of conversation).

[2] **Earnest prayer** - your concern to make disciples will be evident in your prayers (Romans 10:1); the power comes from the Holy Spirit (Acts 1:8).

[3] **Good works** - we are to be people who help others for their own sake but

it is also a means of drawing them to Christ (1 Peter 2:12), as we do it "in the name of the Lord Jesus" (Colossians 3:17) - it gives opportunity to testify. Christ performed miracles, not just to show His divine power, but to help people with real needs. This is a life of self-sacrifice, often of inconvenience, of use of your home and other resources.

[4] **Conversation** - at some point, disciple-making must involve communicating with the individual, usually in conversation. Some guidelines are:

1. show a genuine interest in the other person and their life (rather than talking mostly about yourself) - but don't pry;
2. listen attentively (rather than just thinking about what you are going to say);
3. lead the conversation by asking questions (rather than by preaching, which is threatening) - e.g. "what do you think about..."; "have you ever heard...";
4. introduce spiritual matters and Scripture naturally into the the conversation in context (the Lord often used relevant analogies - e.g. fishing, farming);
5. focus on the person of Christ, not religion, not philosophical debate, etc.;
6. don't try to get too far in one conversation, unless the person wishes to - try to open the way for follow-on conversations;
7. Don't try to 'win' a debate; plant the 'seed' of the Word of God so that the Holy Spirit can do the work in their mind later;
8. Remember you don't have to have an answer for every question on the spot - commit to finding out and getting back to them later;
9. As appropriate, 'witness' as to your own experience and faith;
10. Don't use jargon.

[5] **Invitation** - when they seem ready to accept, invite them to a) your home - for a meal, for further discussion, small group Bible study, etc. (e.g. Acts 18:26) and b) assembly gatherings - e.g. outreach meetings, young peoples' gatherings, to observe the Remembrance (stay with them after the meeting,

introduce them to others, talk to them about the meeting afterwards; they will probably have questions in their minds).

[6] **Offer to help** them on an on-going basis to understand Scripture and its implications - get help from a more experienced disciple if necessary.

f) How to present the gospel:

You may have occasion to present the gospel to one or more people. Following is a suggested outline of what to cover. You may wish to memorize and rehearse it, including key verses. DO NOT APPLY PRESSURE.

[1] **God** (John 3:16)

- God is our Creator;
- He is perfectly holy;
- He loves us;
- His Word (the Bible) is totally authoritative.

[2] **Sin** (Romans 3:23; 6:23)

- we have a sinful nature;
- our sins are against God;
- this sin is serious to God (although we may not think so);
- if not corrected, this sin will result in eternal judgement after our death;
- ignorance is no excuse.

[3] **Christ** (1 Corinthians 15:3; John 3:36)

- Christ is the eternal Son of God;
- He became a man to die for our sins;
- His sacrifice is the only means of salvation from our sin which is acceptable to God.

[4] **Faith** (Ephesians 2:8; Acts 16:31)

· God now commands all people to repent from their sin and put personal faith in Christ;
· Our works, lives, religion, etc. cannot save us.

[5] **Confessing** (Romans 10:9)

· each person, regardless of religious tradition, must confess Christ to God (encourage the person to do this out loud in prayer);
· God assures us in His Word that we are now eternally saved and forgiven;
· All heaven rejoices at a sinner believing.

[6] **Obedience** (2 Corinthians 4:5)

Having received spiritual life, God now calls the believer to the life of a disciple, so that Christ may be both Saviour and Lord to them. Accepting the gospel involves both a person's mind and their heart ("reasoning and persuading" as to the things concerning the kingdom of God - Acts 19:8 RV).

REVIEW QUESTIONS

1. How do people become disciples of the Lord Jesus Christ?
2. Who should make disciples?
3. Why should we make disciples?
4. Of whom should we make disciples?
5. Outline six steps to making a disciple.
6. List several guidelines for carrying on a conversation as a part of disciple-making.
7. Outline six points to cover, with appropriate Scriptures, in presenting the gospel to someone.

MEMORY VERSES

Memorize the following key verses for preaching the gospel: John 3:16; Romans 3:23; Romans 6:23; 1 Corinthians 15:3; Ephesians 2:8; Romans 10:9

DISCUSSION QUESTIONS

1. The Lord testified to Nicodemus, a Jewish ruler, in John 3:1-21, and also to the Samaritan woman in John 4:7-42. Show the similarities and differences in His approach, and how they were applicable to the two situations.
2. 1 Peter 3:15 speaks about being always ready to give an answer. Does this mean we should always wait to be asked before we speak? If not, show this from Scripture.
3. Discuss various ways that you have found to be effective in opening conversations with comparative strangers about spiritual things.
4. Paul said the gospel included (i) repentance toward God, and (ii) faith in the Lord Jesus. Show how the Lord, in John 4, worked to produce both repentance and faith in the Samaritan woman.
5. To what extent should discipleship be evident in a person before they are baptized?
6. Explain (supposedly to a person to whom the gospel message is new) the substitutionary aspect of Christ's death.
7. How would you present the gospel differently to someone who was familiar with the Bible as opposed to someone who wasn't? e.g. Acts 13:16-41 vs. Acts 17.

ASSIGNMENT

During the next week, identify one person whom you would like to see become a disciple of the Lord Jesus, and apply the approach outlined in this session. Make that person a matter of prayer.

12

THE TRIUNE GOD

OBJECTIVES

1. To have a basic understanding of the identity and attributes of the divine Being. 2. To understand the relationship between the three Persons of the Godhead, and their distinctive roles.

ADVANCE READING

Read the following Scriptures and write a brief statement summarizing each: 1. Hebrews 11:6; 2. Psalm 14:1; 3. Romans 1:20,21; 4. 1 Timothy 1:17; 5. Romans 11:33; 6. 1 Peter 1:15; 7. Numbers 23:19; 8. 1 John 4:16; 9. 2 Corinthians 13:14

TOPIC OVERVIEW

a) The nature of God:

- God **exists** (Genesis 1:1; Hebrews 11:6) - the Bible doesn't prove it, it assumes it; it requires faith by man; an atheist doesn't believe it - God says he is a fool (Psalm 14:1); an 'agnostic' doesn't know; but even creation is sufficient evidence for everyone however (Romans 1:21); God is 'self-

existent' – He didn't derive His existence from anyone else;
- God is **unique** (Isaiah 40:18) – no other being is like Him, or can be compared with Him;
- God is **spirit** (John 4:24; Acts 17:24, 25) – His essential being is spiritual, not material;
- God is **divine** (Acts 17:29; Romans 1:20) – is a general term which refers to all his attributes which are in contrast to humanity;
- God is **eternal** (1 Timothy 1:17; Genesis 21:33) – He has neither beginning nor end;
- God is **omniscient** (Job 21:22; Romans 11:33) – He knows everything whether yet known to man or not;
- God is **omnipotent** (Ephesians 1:19; Psalm 147:5) – there is no limit to His ability;
- God is **omnipresent** (Psalm 139:8; Proverbs 15:3) – there is no place to avoid Him;
- God is **perfect** (Matthew 5:48) – He is not lacking in anything;
- God is **infinite** (1 Kings 8:27) – He has no limitations;
- God is **holy** (Isaiah 6:3; 1 Peter 1:15) – He is totally pure;
- God is **sovereign** (Job 9:12; Jude 4) – He has the absolute right to make His own decisions and act as He pleases;
- God is **truthful** (Numbers 23:19; I John 1:5) – He tells the truth, the whole truth, and nothing but the truth. 'God is Truth';
- God is **immutable and consistent** (Hebrews 13:8) – He never changes over time, or varies from day to day (James 1:17);
- God is **love** (1 John 4:16) – He is totally unselfish; everything He does He does in love;
- God is **merciful** (Deuteronomy 4:31; Jeremiah 3:12);
- God **reserves revenge for Himself** (Romans 12:19; Genesis 50:15, 19);
- God is **triune** (Matthew 28:19; 2 Corinthians 13:14) – see below.

b) The purpose of God:

- He established His plan and purpose back in eternity (Ephesians 3:11);
- He chooses human beings to be to the praise of His glory (Ephesians 1:11);
- His purpose always prevails (Proverbs 19:21);
- God exercises His own will to carry out His purposes and pleasure (e.g. James 1:18; Ephesians 1:5);
- God permits us to use our own free will, with the intent that we will choose His will (e.g. Romans 12:2).

c) God the Father:

- is the Father of Jesus, as the Son of God (John 20:17);
- is the Father of believers, who are 'children of God' (John 1:12);
- is located permanently on His throne in heaven (Acts 7:49);
- delights in His Son (2 Peter 1:17);
- can be prayed to as the giver of all things (Matthew 6:6).

d) God the Son:

- is the only begotten Son (John 3:16);
- always was God, continued to be God on earth, and will always be God (John 1:1; Colossians 2:9);
- has been given all authority by His Father (Matthew 28:18);
- glorifies His Father (John 17:4);
- is now in heaven at the right hand of His Father, waiting to return for His saints (Hebrews 1:3);
- took a body when He came to earth ('incarnation'); still has a glorified body in heaven (1 Timothy 3:16).

When He was on earth, He described Himself in many ways, for example:

- **I am the Bread of Life** (John 6:35) - meets the needs of people for eternal life;

- **I am the Truth** (John 14:6) – whatever He said was the truth;
- **I am the Life** (John 11:25; 14:6) – He is the access for disciples (sheep) to the sheepfold (God's house);
- **I am the Light of the World** (John 8:12) – He brings the truth about God to people;
- **I am the Good Shepherd** (John 10:11) – He cares for and gave His life for believers;
- **I am the Son of God** (John 10:36) – He is deity, on equality with God the Father;
- **I am the True Vine** (John 15:1 – He is the source of fruitful lives for believers.

Some of His names and titles are:

- **Lord** – Master, having authority (Acts 2:36);
- **Jesus** – 'God, our Saviour' – his human name (Matthew 1:21);
- **Christ** – 'Messiah' – sent by God (Acts 2:36);
- **Emmanuel** – 'God with us' (Matthew 1:23);
- **High Priest** – over the house of God (Hebrews 2:17).

f) The Trinity in the Old Testament:

The separate identities of the three Persons of the Trinity were not clearly revealed in the Old Testament; they did not use the term 'Father' for God; the identity of the Son of God was not clear although they knew that a Messiah had been promised (John 4:25). All three Persons of the Trinity were involved in creation:

- God (the Father) spoke (Genesis 1:3);
- all things were made through Christ (Colossians 1:16);
- the Spirit moved on the face of the waters (Genesis 1:2).

God identified Himself as Elohim (or El) - Almighty God (the ending 'im' in the Hebrew indicates more than two). Later He identified Himself to Israel as Jehovah - the revealed Lord; for example, in Exodus 6:2,3: "God (Elohim) also said to Moses, 'I am the Lord (Jehovah). I appeared to Abraham, to Isaac and to Jacob as God Almighty (El-Shaddai), but by my name the Lord (Jehovah) I did not make myself known to them.'"

g) The Trinity acting together in the New Testament:

- at the **birth** of Christ: the Father sent the Son, the Son was born as a child, conceived by Mary through the Holy Spirit overshadowing her (Luke 1:35);
- at the **baptism** of Christ: the Father speaking from heaven; "Thou art my beloved Son" (RV); the Son having been baptized in the Jordan; the Holy Spirit descending on Him in the form of a dove (Luke 3:22);
- at the **crucifixion** of Christ: the Father carrying out the judgment on the sin offering; Christ on the cross as the willing sin offering; offering His life through the Holy Spirit to God (Hebrews 9:14);
- in prayer: through Christ (His intercession, and the authority of His name, in which we pray), we have access to the Father, by the Holy Spirit who intercedes within the believer (Ephesians 2:18; Romans 8:26).

REVIEW QUESTIONS

1. List 12 attributes of God.
2. What is 'the purpose of God'?
3. Who are the three Persons of the Godhead?
4. Where is each Person of the Godhead today?
5. Show from Scripture the eternal (past, present, future) deity of Christ.
6. List seven 'I Am' statements of Christ.
7. What is the meaning of each of the three names in the title 'Lord Jesus Christ'?
8. What did Israel know about the Trinity in the Old Testament?
9. How was the Trinity involved at the birth of Christ, His baptism and His

death?

MEMORY VERSE

1 Timothy 1:17 - "Now to the King eternal, immortal, invisible, the only God, be honour and glory for ever and ever."

DISCUSSION QUESTIONS

1. Why do you think some people do not believe in the existence of God?
2. If God is a spirit (John 4:24), what does it mean in Genesis 1:27 that God created man in His own image?
3. Are God's characteristics of love (1 John 4:16) and revengefulness (Romans 12:19) contradictory? Explain.
4. Why did God's eternal purpose involve the human creation being to His praise and glory? (Ephesians 1:5,6)
5. What is the rank of the three Persons of the Trinity?
6. What is the significance of the expression "The God and Father of our Lord Jesus Christ"? (Ephesians 1:3)
7. How do we know that Christ still has a body in heaven?
8. For each of the following 'I Am' statements of Christ, indicate an application to people in the world whereby Christ can meet their needs: a) I am the light of the World, b) I am the Truth, c) I am the Bread of Life, and d) I am the Door.
9. Show how each Person of the Trinity has a distinct role in worship.

ASSIGNMENT

2 Peter 1:3 says that God's divine power has given us 'everything we need...'. Write out a paragraph explaining in practical terms what you think this verse means.

13

THE HOLY SPIRIT (PART 1)

OBJECTIVES

1. To understand that the Holy Spirit is real and is one of the three Persons of the Trinity. 2. To be conscious of how to be filled with the Spirit and how He can be grieved and quenched.

ADVANCE READING

Read the following Scriptures and write a brief summary of the main point of each: 1. Luke 4:1, 14-19; 2. John 7:37-39; 3. John 14:16,17,25,26; 4. John 16:7-15; 5. Acts 1:8; 6. Romans 8:8-17,23-27; 7. 1 Corinthians 6:19; 8. 1 Corinthians 12:13; 9. Galatians 5:22,23; 10. Ephesians 3:16

TOPIC OVERVIEW

In Session 2, we saw that one of the results of your salvation is that God sent His Holy Spirit to permanently indwell you. The purpose of this session is to learn more about the Holy Spirit - who He is, what He does, and how our lives are affected by Him.

a) Who the Holy Spirit is

The Holy Spirit is not just God's influence; He is a distinct Person. When Jesus was speaking here on earth, He continually referred to the Spirit as 'He.' In John 14:16,17, for example, Jesus referred to Him as 'another Counsellor.' The Holy Spirit is one of the three Persons of deity, together with God the Father, and God the Son (Jesus Christ). He is therefore equal with the Father and the Son, but He has a distinct work to do. Acts chapter 5 tells the story of Ananias and Sapphira. How does what it says about Ananias in verses 3 and 4 support the fact that the Holy Spirit is God? Peter equates 'lying to the Holy Spirit' with 'lying to God.'

b) His titles

In the Old Testament, a variety of names was used, such as: the Spirit of God, the Spirit of the Lord, My Spirit, and the Spirit. The New Testament uses an even greater variety, in addition to simply 'The Holy Spirit' (or 'The Holy Ghost'):

- Romans 1:4 - **the Spirit of holiness**;
- Acts 16:7 - **the Spirit of Jesus**;
- 1 Peter 1:11 - **the Spirit of Christ**;
- Hebrews 9:14 - **the eternal Spirit**;
- 2 Corinthians 3:3 - **the Spirit of the living God**;
- 1 Peter 4:14 - **the Spirit of glory**;
- Ephesians 1:13 - **the Holy Spirit of promise** (RV);
- John 14:16,17 - **the Spirit of truth**.

c) His symbols

As you study your Bible, be on the look-out for teaching regarding the Holy Spirit in various symbols. In some cases, He is actually referred to as the symbol; in others, it is just used to illustrate His person or work:

- Acts 2:3 - **fire** = holiness;
- Matthew 3:16 - **dove** = gentleness;
- Zechariah 4:6,11-14 - **oil** = fuel for light for a testimony;
- John 3:8 - **wind** = invisibility;
- Exodus 13:21 - **cloud** = heavenly guide.

d) His work in the Old Testament

What activities did the Holy Spirit engage in during the time of the Old Testament?

- Genesis 1:2 - creation;
- Acts 1:16 - inspiration of Scripture;
- Judges 14:6 - empowering men for service.

e) His work with Christ on the Earth

During Christ's lifetime, how was the Spirit involved?

- Luke 1:35 - at Christ's birth;
- Luke 3:22; 4:1 - at His baptism;
- Luke 4:14-18 - in His ministry;
- Hebrews 9:14 - in His death;
- Romans 8:11 - in His resurrection.

f) His work today with unbelievers

In John 16:8-11, Jesus described what the work of the Holy Spirit would be with unbelievers, as follows:

- He convicts them of the sin of unbelief in Christ;
- He convicts them of their lack of the righteousness of Christ;
- He convicts them of the inevitability of future judgement.

g) His work at salvation

The Holy Spirit plays a large part in the salvation of a sinner. Following are six effects of the Spirit's work:

1. **Born of the Spirit** (John 3:6-8) - the new birth takes place by the Spirit using the Word of God in our hearts;
2. **Baptized in the Spirit** (1 Corinthians 12:13; John 1:33) - the Lord Jesus immersed us spiritually in the Holy Spirit to make us a member of the Church the Body of Christ;
3. **Indwelt by the Spirit** (Romans 8:9; John 14:17) - previously the Holy Spirit was 'with' people; now He permanently indwells;
4. **Sealed with the Spirit** (Ephesians 1:13) - we are identified as belonging to Christ, and secured for salvation;
5. **Received a pledge of the Spirit** (2 Corinthians 1:22; Ephesians 1:14) - He is the prepayment, or advance deposit, to guarantee our possession by God;
6. **Anointed with the Spirit** (1 John 2:20) - we are anointed with the Holy Spirit for service.

h) His work today with believers

The Holy Spirit is the person of God who gives effect to the reality of Christian life.For example:

- we walk by the Spirit (Galatians 5:16,17,25) - that is, He enables us to live a disciple life; He gives victory over our human nature;
- we are told to be filled with the Spirit (Ephesians 5:18) - to be totally under His control;
- we are not to grieve Him (Ephesians 4:30) or insult Him (Hebrews 10:29);
- we are not to quench His work within us, since He will not force Himself against our will.

To the extent we have this on-going experience of walking in the Spirit, He will carry out the following functions for us:

- He will **teach** us the truth of God (John 14:26);
- He will **comfort and counsel** us (John 14:16,17,26);
- He will **guide and lead** us in our decisions (John 16:13);
- He will **empower** us for service for the Lord (Acts 1:8; Ephesians 3:16);
- He will **intercede** for us in our prayers (Romans 8:26,27);
- He will **glorify Christ** in our lives (John 16:14);
- He will **produce fruit** in our lives (Galatians 5:22,23).

REVIEW QUESTIONS

1. What was the difference between the Holy Spirit's presence with a person before and after Pentecost?
2. How would you prove the Holy Spirit is God?
3. Give six of the titles of the Holy Spirit in the New Testament.
4. One of the Holy Spirit's works today is as teacher. Give six other ways in which He serves.
5. What is the difference between being baptized in the Holy Spirit and being filled with the Spirit?
6. What two lessons would you particularly learn from being 'sealed' with the Spirit?
7. In what way does the Holy Spirit work in unsaved people?
8. List four of the symbols to which the Holy Spirit is likened.

MEMORY VERSE

1 Corinthians 6:19 - "Do you not know that your body is a temple of the Holy Spirit, who is in you, whom you have received from God? You are not your own; you were bought at a price. Therefore honour God with your body."

DISCUSSION QUESTIONS

1. In John 14:16,26; 16:7, the Lord Jesus described the Holy Spirit with the word 'Paraclete', which is variously translated as Comforter, Helper, Counsellor, Advocate. What can we learn from these various meanings?

2. Ephesians 4:30 tells us to not grieve the Holy Spirit. From the verses before and after that, what can we learn about how the Holy Spirit is grieved?

3. The Lord Jesus taught his disciples about the Holy Spirit in the upper room the night before his death, in John chapters 14 and 16. In chapter 15, he spoke about bearing fruit (e.g. John 15:16). Is this the same fruit as is referred to in Galatians 5:22,23? How is it produced?

4. In Acts 1:8, the Lord Jesus promised that the Holy Spirit would give power for witness. From Acts 4:31, Ephesians 3:16 and Philippians 4:13, in what ways does He empower us?

ASSIGNMENT

Baptism in the Holy Spirit is referred to by some people as an experience which comes later, if at all, after salvation, and one which Christians should pray to receive as a 'second blessing.' What Scriptures would you use to show that this is not true, and how could you properly respond to someone who stated this?

14

THE HOLY SPIRIT (PART 2)

OBJECTIVES

1. To understand the gifts of the Holy Spirit and those which apply to us today.
2. To be helped to determine what my gift is and how I can develop it.

ADVANCE READING

Read the following Scriptures and write a brief statement summarizing each one: 1. 1 Corinthians 12:1-11; 2. Romans 12:6-8; 3. Ephesians 4:7-16; 4. Hebrews 2:4

TOPIC OVERVIEW

When the Lord Jesus told His apostles that the Holy Spirit would come, after He had returned to heaven, He described the Spirit as "power from on high." And so the work that the Spirit was going to do was not going to be done alone, it was going to be done through believers. The Holy Spirit does this by giving 'spiritual gifts' to all believers, to empower them for the work of God.

a) 1 Corinthians 12:4,11

What do these verses teach us about these gifts? They are all different but come through the same Holy Spirit. What are the particular gifts referred to in verses 8 to 10 of this chapter? 1. wisdom 2. knowledge 3. faith 4. healing 5. miraculous powers 6. prophecy 7. ability to distinguish spirits 8. tongues 9. interpretation of tongues

b) Romans 12:6-8

What gifts are mentioned in Romans 12:6-8? Prophesying, serving; teaching; encouraging; giving; leading; showing mercy. What is the main point that is being made about the gifts in these verses? Using the gift to the full.

c) Ephesians 4:7-16

Which believers have been given spiritual gifts? Each one - see verse 7. What is the purpose of these gifts? "To prepare God's people for works of service, so that the body of Christ may be built up until we all reach unity in the faith and in the knowledge of the Son of God and become mature, attaining to the whole measure of the fulness of Christ" (vv.12-13). Verse 11 identifies some of the men in the early churches of God who used certain spiritual gifts. How are they referred to? Apostles, prophets, evangelists, pastors, teachers.

d) Miraculous gifts

Some of the gifts referred to in these chapters were miraculous in nature. Miraculous powers were given to the apostles and some others in the early churches, before the New Testament was completed, as 'signs' to establish that what they were teaching was truly from God. Hebrews 2:4 (KJV): "God also bearing them witness, both with signs and wonders and with divers miracles, and gifts of the Holy Ghost, according to his own will." The two most common types of miraculous powers were "speaking in tongues" and "faith healing." Do these apply today?

e) Speaking in tongues

"Speaking in tongues" refers to speaking in a language which is unknown to the speaker. There are three occurrences of this in the book of the Acts:

1. ch.2 – at Pentecost; on this occasion the languages were known by the audience, and this enabled them to understand this first gospel message;
2. ch.10 – by Cornelius, the first Gentile believer, who spoke in tongues while praising God, after receiving salvation;
3. ch.19 – in Europe; they spoke in tongues while prophesying.

Most references to tongues are in 1 Corinthians, which is an epistle which was written to the Church at Corinth to correct a lot of problems. The writer, the apostle Paul, refers to tongues in chapters 12 to 14. What does he say in the following verses?

- 14:37 – "What I am writing to you is the Lord's command";
- 12:30 – "Do all work miracles?; Do all have gifts of healing?; Do all speak in tongues?; Do all interpret?";
- 13:8 – "where there are tongues, they will be stilled (cease)";
- 14:22 – "Tongues, then, are a sign, not for believers but for unbelievers";
- 14:28 – "If there is no interpreter, the speaker should keep quiet in the church."

Although in the early days of the New Testament speaking in tongues was a sign that the Holy Spirit had been given, it was not evidence of having received salvation; not all who were saved spoke in tongues. They were a lesser gift, given for the apostolic period of time, as evidence of the divine authority of what the apostles taught, until the New Testament Scriptures were completed. Tongues are not evidence of a 'second blessing', or 'baptism of the Holy Spirit', as is sometimes referred to. 1 Corinthians 12:13 (RV): "For in one Spirit were we all baptized into one body."

f) Faith healing

As with the miraculous gift of speaking in tongues, the apostles and others had this gift during the apostolic period. Again, it was evidence to others of their divine authority (see Mark 16:17,18).The gift of healing in those days:

- included raising the dead (for example: Dorcas in Acts 9:36-41);
- was instantaneous and complete (for example: the cripple in Acts 3:7);
- was not dependent on the degree of the patient's own faith (for example: the demon- possessed boy in Mark 9:22-24);
- was not exercised indiscriminately (for example: Paul left Trophimus sick at Miletus in 2 Timothy 4:20) and did not heal him.

For today, the instructions to us are (James 5:16) to pray one for another that the sick may be healed. We should examine ourselves to see if the sickness is the result of divine judgement (1 Corinthians 11:30,31). There is no evidence today of faith healers picking up serpents and drinking deadly poison in a present-day fulfilment of the remainder of Mark 16:17,18.

REVIEW QUESTIONS

1. Who has received a spiritual gift?
2. Who distributes the gift?
3. What are some of the gifts that apply today?
4. What was the purpose in the early days of miraculous gifts?
5. When does baptism in the Holy Spirit take place?

MEMORY VERSE

Hebrews 2:4 - "God also testified to it by signs, wonders and various miracles, and gifts of the Holy Spirit distributed according to his will."

DISCUSSION QUESTIONS

1. The gifts given by the Holy Spirit are many and varied. They are to be mutually helpful and interdependent. How and where are these gifts to be used?
2. Timothy was encouraged to 'stir up' the gift that was in him (2 Timothy 1:6). What are some practical ways of doing this?

ASSIGNMENT

In what ways can you discover which spiritual gift(s) the Holy Spirit has given you? Discuss this with other disciples.

15

FUTURE EVENTS

OBJECTIVES

1. To understand the general sequence of future events, according to Scripture, and their relevance to believers and unbelievers. 2. To have an increased awareness of the soon coming of the Lord Jesus.

ADVANCE READING

Read the following Scriptures and write a brief statement summarizing each one: 1. 1 Thessalonians 4:13-5:5; 2. 2 Thessalonians 2:1-12; 3. 2 Peter 3:3-13; 4. Hebrews 10:37; 5. John 14:1-3

TOPIC OVERVIEW

a) When will these events occur?

We can't be sure of the exact timing – "of that day and hour knoweth no one, not even the angels of heaven, neither the Son, but the Father only" (Matthew 24:36 RV). However, we know that these are "the last days" (Matthew 24:37; 2 Timothy 3:1-5; 2 Peter 3:3-13).

b) The 'Rapture' (1 Thessalonians 4:13-17):

It is the first event to occur; there are no unfulfilled prophecies to precede it; it is not a scriptural term; it means 'to be caught up.' Believers (alive and dead, raised to life) will together be caught up to meet the Lord in the air (1 Thessalonians 4:13-18). It is for those 'in Christ' - not the unsaved - this will be a private coming for believers (Matthew 24) (in contrast to (e) below); the unsaved will not see it. There will be: a shout, the voice of the archangel and the trump of God.

Those who have died 'in Christ' will be resurrected; those who are living 'in Christ' will have their bodies made incorruptible "in the twinkling of an eye" (Philippians 3:20,21; 2 Corinthians 5:1-5; Romans 7:24; 2 Corinthians 15:51-55). We should be looking forward to this (2 Timothy 4:8), and it should influence our conduct now (2 Peter 3:11). We will never leave Him after this. It will take place in the air.

c) The Judgement Seat of Christ (2 Corinthians 5:10; Romans 14:12; 1 Corinthians 3:13; 4:5):

It is for believers, for the Lord to evaluate their service for Him. It is not for punishment of sins, before or after salvation (Romans 8:1). Each person will have to give an account to the Lord. The outcome for each Christian will be reward or loss of his life-work (but not vengeance on others).Overseers will also have to give an account for the saints under their care (Hebrews 13:17) for their benefit or loss.

d) The Great Tribulation (Revelation 6-18):

It is a period of 3 1/2 years on the earth, after the Rapture (Daniel 9:26,27); probably, it will be taking place on earth while the Judgement Seat is occurring in the air. It will be a time of terrible evil and natural disasters, especially the last three and a half years, and especially in Israel - it is "the time of Jacob's trouble" (Jeremiah 30:7 RV). A world leader will arise - called "The Beast." He will make a covenant with Israel, but break it after the first three and a half years (Daniel 9:27).

He will force people to wear his mark (the number 666) in order to buy and sell, and also to worship him, and will kill those who don't (Revelation 13:16-18). When Israel sees an image of the Beast in their temple in Jerusalem, they will escape to mountains in three countries east of Israel (Daniel 11:41).It will be a time of great activity by Satan, referred to as 'the dragon' (e.g. Revelation 12:13) -compare the serpent in the Garden of Eden. It will be possible to be saved from this tribulation, but only by being a martyr (Revelation 7:9,14).

e) The Second Coming of Christ (2 Thessalonians 1:7-10):

This will be His public appearing on the earth (Revelation 1:7). His first coming was in humility; this will be in glory. He will come to the Mount of Olives, east of Jerusalem, which is where He left from (Acts 1:11); it will split in two, east and west (Zechariah 14:4). We shall come with Him, in the clouds. His coming begins "the day of the Lord."

f) The Battle of Armageddon (Revelation 16:16):

It will be a brief but fierce battle between the armies of the earth and 'the Lamb' (i.e. Christ) (Revelation 17:14; 19:19). It will take place in the valley of Megiddo in northern Israel (just south of Nazareth). The blood will flow for 180 miles four feet deep. The Lord will destroy them with "the breath of His mouth."

g) The Judgement of the living nations (Joel 3:2):

It will take place in the valley of Jehoshaphat, just south of Jerusalem. The Lord will judge the nations because of their mistreatment of Israel (Zechariah 2:8) and their own wickedness (John 3:19). God has committed all judgement to His Son (John 5:22). Matthew 25:31-46 describes this judgement; those who have treated the Jews well will be welcomed to eternal life; those who have mistreated them will be banished to the Lake of Fire –see (i) below.

h) The Millennium (Revelation 20:1-10; Isaiah 11):

It is a reign of 1000 years by Christ over the earth, from Jerusalem. He will take His rightful place as the heir to king David's throne (2 Samuel 7; Luke 1:32,33). All the earth will be "in subjection under his feet" (Hebrews 2:6-8 RV). We will be part of His government (2 Timothy 2:12; 1 Corinthians 6:2). He will rule with an iron hand; He will tolerate no disobedience. Satan will have been chained up in a pit during this time; although his influence is removed, sin will still exist, showing that sin comes from within man, not just because of his environment. When Satan is released at the end of the 1000 years, he will gather the nations together and attempt to overthrow Jerusalem, where Christ reigns, but fire will come down to prevent it; Satan and his angels will be thrown into the Lake of Fire, which was made for them, for ever.

i) Great White Throne (Revelation 20:11-15):

This is the final judgement of all those not already judged (or those exempt – 'in Christ'). The dead will be raised to be judged (see Hebrews 9:27). The 'book of life', which records the names of all believers (Luke 10:20), will be opened; anyone whose name is not written there will be condemned to the Lake of Fire which is eternal punishment; this is the 'second death.'

j) The new heaven and earth (Revelation 21,22):

After this final judgement, the universe will be dissolved with fire (2 Peter 3:10-13). The new heaven and earth will contain the new city of Jerusalem - the city of gold. It will be inhabited by all those who have been saved by faith in all dispensations of time (Hebrews 11:16; 13:14). Finally, Christ, having been victorious over all His enemies, will transfer all authority back to His

Father, that "God may be all in all" (1 Corinthians 15:24-28).

REVIEW QUESTIONS

1. What are the nine major future events, in sequence?
2. What (if any) prophecy is yet to be fulfilled before the Lord returns to the air for the church which is His body?
3. What will be the results of the Judgement Seat of Christ?
4. What is the Millennium and where will it take place?
5. Who will be at the Great White Throne? Will you be there?6. What is "the day of the Lord"?
6. Who are "the beast", "the antiChrist" and "the dragon"?

MEMORY VERSE

1 Thessalonians 4:16,17 - "For the Lord himself will come down from heaven, with a loud command, with the voice of the archangel and with the trumpet call of God, and the dead in Christ will rise first. After that, we who are still alive and are left will be caught up together with them in the clouds to meet the Lord in the air. And so we will be with the Lord for ever."

DISCUSSION QUESTIONS

1. What is the difference between the Judgement Seat of Christ and the Great White Throne Judgement?
2. Describe the Battle of Armageddon, and find its location on a map. (Zechariah 14:1-3; Revelation 16:12-16; Revelation 19:11-20; Matthew 24:29).
3. How do we know that Christians will not go through the Tribulation? (Compare: 1 Thessalonians 4:15-18; 2 Thessalonians 2:1-12; Daniel 8:9-14; 9:24-27).
4. What are the four things which will not exist in the New Jerusalem (Revelation 21) and why will there be no need for them?

5. Describe what will happen at the Judgement Seat of Christ (from 2 Corinthians 5:10; Romans 14:12; 1 Corinthians 3:13; 1 Corinthians 4:5; Revelation 3:11).

ASSIGNMENT

Draw a time chart showing the sequence and duration of the nine major future events described in this chapter.

16

THE CHURCH THE BODY OF CHRIST

OBJECTIVES

1. To understand the unique privilege that all believers in Christ have. 2. To understand the difference between the Body of Christ and a church of God.

ADVANCE READING

Read the following Scriptures and write a brief statement summarizing what each one says about the Church the Body of Christ: 1. Matthew 16:13-18; 2. Ephesians 3:4-6,9; 3. Ephesians 4:4; 4. Ephesians 4:11-13; 5. Ephesians 4:15,16; 6. Ephesians 5:25,26; 7. Ephesians 5:30; 8. Ephesians 5:31,32

TOPIC OVERVIEW

a) A new revelation

In Matthew 16:13-19, Christ announced for the first time a plan that God had had since before the world was created; that all people (whether Jew or Gentile) who believed in Christ, should be united to form a unique group called "the Church (congregation) which is the body of Christ"; in effect, when His bodily presence would no longer be here on earth, believers would be His bodily presence.

Peter had just confessed Jesus to be "the Christ, the Son of the living God," and this confession of faith was to be the basis ('the rock') on which this new 'church' was to be built; Peter's faith was based on a revelation by God, not from other people ("this was not revealed to you by man, but by my Father in heaven" Matthew 16:17).

A believer becomes a member of this Body at the instant of his or her salvation, by being baptized by Christ in the Holy Spirit into this Body (John 1:33; 1 Corinthians 12:13); this is not the same as water baptism; Jesus also said that this Church would last for ever and could not be spoiled by Satan - another assurance that we cannot lose our salvation.

b) Who are members of this Church?

The Church the Body of Christ consists of all believers in Christ (all who are 'in Christ'), regardless of whatever church on earth they attend (2 Corinthians 5:17). Because no one other than God knows who are all in it, it is invisible; it won't become visible until the entire church (both those who have been dead and those who are living) meets Christ at 'the Rapture' (see Colossians 3:3,4).

This church came into existence at Pentecost, 10 days after the final ascension of Christ, when about 3000 souls received Peter's preaching (Acts 2:41). Even in Old Testament times there had been suggestions of it, which we can now understand with hindsight; for example, in Genesis 24 - Rebekah (the church) was obtained by the father (the Father) to be a bride for Isaac (the Lord Jesus). Christ first announced it in Matthew 16 to His disciples, telling them that He would build it.

c) Ephesians chapters 3 to 5:

The apostle Paul explained it in some of his epistles, especially Ephesians:

- 3:3-6 - that both Gentiles and Jews should be united in this 'Body' had been a mystery which was now revealed;
- 3:10,11 – God's wise purpose would be understood by the angels of heaven when they saw this Church;
- 3:21 - the Church should glorify God;
- 4:4 - there is just one Church the Body;
- 4:11-13 - men with various gifts were given so that the Church might be built up - to reach unity in the faith and maturity in the knowledge of Christ;
- 4:15,16 - Christ is the Head of this Body (also Ephesians 5:23); the Church must submit to Him;
- 5:25,26 - Christ loved the Church and gave Himself up for her, to make her holy;
- 5:30 - believers are members of His Body; there are no distinctions among them (Galatians 3:28);
- 5:31,32 - marriage on earth is an illustration of the union between Christ and His Church.

d) Distinction from the churches of God

The Church the Body of Christ is not the same thing as the churches of God in the house of God. Confusion about this fact is what has led many believers into various denominations rather than into churches of God.

A COMPARISON OF THE CHURCH THE BODY (CTB) AND CHURCHES OF GOD (COG)

1. CTB = heavenly, invisible; COG = on earth, visible;
2. CTB = is perfect in Christ; COG = are imperfect;
3. CTB = is only one; COG = are many, in different locations linked in fellowship;
4. CTB = began at Pentecost and is eternal; COG = began at Pentecost, but can end;
5. CTB = believers are baptized (in Spirit); COG = believers are baptized (in water);
6. CTB = disciples are added to it automatically; COG = believers must be added;
7. CTB = it cannot be damaged; COG = they can be persecuted and damaged;
8. CTB = it has no need for discipline or judgement; COG = discipline and judgement must be carried out in them;
9. CTB = no male/female distinctions; COG = men and women have different roles in them;
10. CTB = no distinctions in status; COG = there are recognized leaders in them;
11. CTB = consists of those who are 'in Christ'; COG = consists of those who are 'in the Lord';
12. CTB = no one can leave it or be put out; those added can leave or be put out of it.

A believer who is in a true - biblical - church of God is also in the Church the Body of Christ; but not all believers are in churches of God.

REVIEW QUESTIONS

1. To whom did Christ first reveal the 'mystery' of the Church the Body of Christ
2. Who comprise the Church the Body?

3. When did it begin? When will it end?
4. What is meant by the Lord's words: 'the gates of Hades will not overcome it' in Matthew 16:18?
5. What are four differences between the Church the Body and the churches of God?
6. What is the position of Christ and of believers in this Church?
7. Why were spiritual gifts given to the Church?
8. What will happen to the Church at the 'rapture'?

MEMORY VERSE

Ephesians 5:25,26,30 - "... Christ loved the church and gave Himself up for her to make her holy, cleansing her by the washing with water through the word... we are members of his body."

DISCUSSION QUESTIONS

1. In what way was the truth of the Church the Body of Christ a 'mystery'? (Ephesians 3:9)
2. Compare baptism in the Holy Spirit at salvation with baptism of a believer in water. (Refer for an illustration to 1 Corinthians 10:2).
3. Show how the Church the Body of Christ and churches of God cannot be the same thing.
4. Describe the relationship between Christ and believers, and among believers, in the Church the Body of Christ.
5. How did the introduction of the Church the Body of Christ unite Jews and Gentiles? (Ephesians 2:14, 15)

ASSIGNMENT

Search online for content on the Church the Body of Christ and identify where it assumes that the Church the Body and the local church on earth are the same. Show from Scripture how it should be corrected.

17

THE CHURCHES OF GOD

OBJECTIVES

1. To understand that God's purpose for disciples is that they should be associated together, rather than remain independent, to be obedient to the commands of the Lord Jesus. 2. To appreciate that, for a disciple who has been taught these things, being in a church of God is expected of him or her since there are no scriptural alternatives.

ADVANCE READING

Read the following Scriptures and write a brief statement summarizing each: 1. John 17:21,22; 2. Psalm 133:1; 3. Acts 2:41,42; 4. Jude v.3; 5. 1 Corinthians 1:9; 6. 1 Timothy 3:15

TOPIC OVERVIEW

a) Disciples should be gathered together:

God does not intend believers in Christ to be isolated or independent. He wants them to be associated together - to be 'one' (John 17:21,22); He wants visible unity rather than individualism (Psalm 133:1; 1 Corinthians 1:10). The practical reasons for this are:

- for mutual teaching and encouragement (1 Timothy 4:11);
- for collective service using our differing abilities - i.e. teamwork (1 Corinthians 12:4-11);
- to require humility and subjection (1 Peter 5:5).

b) God has prescribed how disciples should be gathered together:

It is not on the basis of the salvation we share with all believers, but on adherence to the teaching ('doctrine') of the Lord Jesus. Christ told His apostles to "go ... make disciples ... baptising them ... teaching them to observe ALL things whatsoever I have commanded you" (Matthew 28:19,20 RV). The first time the apostles did this, ten days later at Pentecost, those who believed were baptized and they "continued stedfastly in the apostles' teaching" (Acts 2:42 RV). This teaching from Christ, taught by the apostles, became known as 'the faith,' which was taught in its entirety to the saints (Jude v.3).

Advising believers to 'go to the church of their choice' is not scriptural. God has chosen our church for us - the church of God. Such churches must conform to the pattern of New Testament teaching for churches of God.

c) The New Testament churches:

The first time the gospel was preached after Christ's resurrection was in Jerusalem at Pentecost by the apostle Peter (Acts 2:41,42). The result was that about 3000 people [1] received his word (were saved) [2] were baptized [3] were added to the 120 disciples already gathered there continued steadfastly in: [4] the apostles' doctrine, [5] the Fellowship, [6] the breaking of bread (Remembrance), [7] the prayers. This was the beginning of 'the Church of God in Jerusalem' (Acts 11:22). As the gospel spread, more believers were baptized and churches of God were established in various cities, for example: Antioch (Acts 13:1); Caesarea (Acts 18:22); Ephesus (Acts 20:17); Cenchrea (Romans 16:1); and Corinth (1 Corinthians 1:2).

These churches consisted of 'saints' some of whom were 'deacons' and some were 'overseers' (Philippians 1:1). These local churches of God together formed 'the fellowship of his Son' (1 Corinthians 1:9 RV) and 'the house of God' (Ephesians 2:21,22).

c) The New Testament churches:

The word 'church' is 'ecclesia' in Greek - it means 'called out together'. Local churches of God are different from the one 'Church the Body of Christ' consisting of all believers (refer to Session 16). A church is the people (congregation), not the building where they meet.

d) Terminology:

The New Testament uses the following expressions:

- **'the church of God'** - the congregation of those in the house of God who are in the city (e.g. 1 Corinthians 1:2);
- **'the Fellowship'** - the community of all the saints in all churches of God worldwide (e.g. 1 Corinthians 1:9);
- **'the house of God'** - the churches of God together, among whom God dwells (1 Timothy 3:15);
- **'saints'** (always plural) – **'holy ones'** - those whom God has sanctified and are in churches of God (1 Corinthians 14:33);
- **'the kingdom of God'** - the people in the churches of God, over whom the Lord Jesus Christ has authority (e.g. Acts 1:3);

- **'the Flock'** - a symbolic expression, referring to the people as sheep gathered together under the chief shepherd (e.g. 1 Peter 5:2,4);
- **'the people of God'** - those in the churches of God, as a holy nation separated to God for his own possession (e.g. 1 Peter 2:10);
- **'holy priesthood'** - those in the house of God in their service towards other people (e.g. preaching the gospel) (1 Peter 2:9);
- **'in the Lord'** - the relationship of those in the Kingdom of God (different from 'in Christ' which describes all believers) (e.g. 1 Thessalonians 5:12);
- **'the Faith'** - the complete teaching of the Lord Jesus, taught by His apostles (e.g. Jude 3);
- **'churches of Christ'** - i.e. churches of God demonstrating Christ-like character (Romans 16:16);
- **'churches of the saints'** - (1 Corinthians 14:33 RV).

REVIEW QUESTIONS

1. How did Christ express God's desire that believers should be visibly united, in His prayer in John 17?
2. What are three practical reasons for believers to be associated in a collective way?
3. Should the basis of association be salvation or obedience to Christ's teaching?
4. What is the name of the group to which believers should be joined?
5. What is the prerequisite for a believer to be added to a church of God?
6. Is any church with Christians a church of God?
7. Name some churches of God in the New Testament.
8. What do the following expressions mean - ecclesia, house of God, kingdom of God, people of God?
9. Are the same people in the churches of God, House of God, Kingdom of God, and people of God?
10. 10. Contrast being 'in the Lord' with being 'in Christ.'

MEMORY VERSE

Acts 2:41,42 - "Those then who accepted his message were baptised, and about three thousand were added to their number that day. They devoted themselves to the apostles' teaching and to the fellowship, to the breaking of bread and to prayer."

DISCUSSION QUESTIONS

1. What are some of the differences between the early churches of God in the New Testament and churches of God today?
2. Following is a 'chain of logic' which shows that the bolded terms all refer to the same people. From the scriptures listed below, select the scripture which helps to show that each statement in this chain is true:

- 1) baptized disciples should be added to a **church of God...**
- 2) whereby they are in the **kingdom of God...**
- 3) which was given to the **little Flock...**
- 4) which are under overseers in the **church of God...**
- 5) the overseers and churches are in the **house of God...**
- 6) which functions in worship as a **priesthood...**
- 7) which consists of the **people of God...**
- 8) which is a **temple of God...**
- 9) which consists of **several buildings...**
- 10) which are each **churches of God.**

Scriptures: Luke 12:32; Acts 11:26; Acts 14:22, 23; Acts 20:28; 1 Corinthians 3:9; 2 Corinthians 6:16; Ephesians 2:21,22; 1 Timothy 3:2,5,15; 1 Peter 2:5; 1 Peter 2:9,10

ASSIGNMENT

Review websites of some local churches and identify things referred to which do not correspond to a scriptural church of God.

18

THE HOUSE OF GOD (PART 1)

OBJECTIVES

1. To understand who the house of God is today. 2. To understand the divine service of the house of God.

ADVANCE READING

Read the following Scriptures and write a brief statement summarizing each one: 1. 1 Peter 2:1-10; 2. 1 Corinthians 11:23-30; 3. Hebrews 10:19-22; 4. Hebrews 4:14-16

TOPIC OVERVIEW

a) God's dwelling place:

God desires to dwell (live) among His people. This is one of the reasons why He has called disciples together in churches of God. 1 Peter 2 describes the process:

- v.3 - believers who have experienced the grace of God in salvation...

- v.2 - ...grow up in their salvation (discipleship) through application of the Word of God and ...
- v.4 - they come to the Lord like living stones to be built into the house which is built around Him as the chief corner-stone;
- v.5 - the individual stones are built up and established into the one and only house of God, which is His holy temple. The house of God is the place on earth where God can live among His people. There can only be one house of God on earth at one time.

b) A place of service:

The House of God is a place of divine service - in two directions: *worship to God* (1 Peter 2:5 – 'a holy priesthood') *showing forth to people* (1 Peter 2:9 – 'a royal priesthood'). This is the same priesthood, doing two different things. Service in the house of God is the service of a priesthood. Christ is the Great Priest over the house of God (Hebrews 4:14; 10:21). He does not have that function for believers who are not in the house of God.

The primary gatherings of a church of God to engage in this service are Remembrance and worship, Prayers, Gospel preaching; and Ministry of the Word. It is not possible to carry out this priesthood service as an individual believer or other than in the house of God. Those in the house of God (the churches of God) are therefore exhorted to gather together (Hebrews 10:25).

c) Remembrance and worship:

It takes place every week (Acts 20:7) and is the first thing done on the first day of the week, since the Lord should get our first and best (Proverbs 3:9). (The first day of the week is resurrection day - e.g. John 20:1). It begins with the 'remembrance' of the death and resurrection of the Lord Jesus in the symbols of breaking and eating bread and pouring out and drinking wine (1 Corinthians 11:23-30).

The bread symbolizes the body of the Lord that He offered to God on Calvary as a sinless offering. The wine symbolizes the blood of the Lord that was poured out as atonement for sin. It is a 'closed table', in that those in churches of God only may participate.It then continues with brothers leading the assembly in speaking to God in worship and thanksgiving for Christ, ("the fruit of lips which make confession to his name" - Hebrews 13:15 RV), and in giving out hymns of praise for Christ which the assembly sing (from the first section of the hymnbook 'Psalms, Hymns & Spiritual Songs' - see Ephesians 5:19).

Any brother in the assembly (unless he is under discipline) can lead the assembly in this way; a sister cannot lead, but should join in the singing and in worshipping silently (1 Corinthians 14:26, 34; 1 Timothy 2:8). All should say Amen (1 Corinthians 14:16).This worship is not just an activity of individual churches of God but a united action of the entire house of God entering in Spirit into God's intimate presence as a holy priesthood (Hebrews 10:19-22).

d) The Prayers

The house of God is intended to be a place of prayer (Mark 11:17). The first Church of God in Jerusalem "continued stedfastly in the prayers" (Acts 2:42 RV; Acts 12:5). The united prayer of God's people is important to God (Matthew 18:19; Acts 1:14; 1 Timothy 2:1-4). This collective prayer is in addition to individual prayer (refer to Session 7). The people of God draw near to God at 'the throne of grace' to get help in time of need (Hebrews 4:14-16). It was symbolized in the tabernacle and temples in the Old Testament by the incense that was burned on the golden altar (Revelation 5:8; Exodus 30:1,7; Luke 1:10).

e) The gospel ('the good news'):

Churches of God are symbolized by the golden lampstand in the Tabernacle (Revelation 1:20; Exodus 25:31); they are to be a testimony to God in their locality, showing forth the excellencies of Christ as a royal priesthood (1 Peter 2:9); this involves preaching the gospel (1 Thessalonians 1:8). This involves the use of the gift of evangelism (Acts 21:8; 2 Timothy 4:5) The gospel includes not only salvation but "the whole counsel of God" (Acts 20:27 RV) involving the lordship of Christ, discipleship, the house of God, etc. This collective preaching of the gospel as a royal priesthood is in addition to individual witnessing. It can involve regular gospel meetings, special gospel campaigns, open-air gospel preaching, Sunday Schools, camps, radio broadcasts, distribution of literature, etc.

f) Ministry of the Word:

The apostles taught the commandments of the Lord. It was known as "the apostles' teaching" (Acts 2:42). They emphasized it as an important activity (Acts 6:4). Ministry of the Word is to be done today in churches of God by brothers capable of doing so (James 3:1; 1 Peter 4:10,11). It should be an important activity of the church because of the need to build one another up in the Faith. It consists of:

- exposition (explanation) of the Scriptures;
- teaching of doctrine from the Scriptures (2 Timothy 3:16);
- reminding the saints of the Scriptures (1 Timothy 4:6);
- sharing devotional thoughts about Christ from the Scriptures.

The apostle Paul both taught orally in person and wrote epistles to churches of God. Today, ministry of the Word in churches of God is similarly complemented by written ministry. - e.g. Needed Truth magazine for teaching of Scripture and Bible Studies magazine for discussion ('exploration') of Scripture.

REVIEW QUESTIONS

1. What comprises the spiritual house of God?
2. What are the two kinds of priestly service that take place in the house of God?

3. What meetings are convened for holy priesthood service?
4. What are Christ's titles in relation to the house of God (Hebrews 3:6; 10:21)?
5. What meetings are convened for royal priesthood service?
6. Can an individual believer engage in holy or royal priesthood service?
7. When should the Remembrance be held?
8. What do the bread and wine symbolize?
9. Who can lead the assembly in thanksgiving and giving out hymns during the Remembrance?
10. Where do the people of God come to spiritually in the prayers?
11. What item in the Tabernacle in the Old Testament symbolized the people as being a testimony for God on earth?
12. What does 'the gospel' include?
13. Why is ministry of the Word important?

MEMORY VERSE

1 Peter 2:5 - "...you also, like living stones, are being built into a spiritual house to be a holy priesthood, offering spiritual sacrifices acceptable to God through Jesus Christ."

DISCUSSION QUESTIONS

1. How can you prepare for the Remembrance each week?
2. Describe our entrance into the holies (Hebrews 10:19-22).
3. Explain Ephesians 2:19-22 in your own words.
4. What are the essential points that should be covered in preaching the gospel?
5. What is God's attitude to churches other than churches of God?

ASSIGNMENT

Make a special point this week of preparing your thoughts for next Lord's Day's Remembrance meeting.

19

THE HOUSE OF GOD (PART 2)

OBJECTIVES

1. To understand who the house of God is today. 2. To understand the divine service of the house of God.

ADVANCE READING

Read the following Scriptures and write a brief statement summarizing each one: 1. Ephesians 4:7-13; 2. 1 Corinthians 12:1-11; 3. 1 Peter 4:10; 4. Ephesians 5:19,20; 5. 2 Corinthians 9:6-8; 6. Luke 6:38; 7. 1 Corinthians 16:1

TOPIC OVERVIEW

a) Spiritual gifts:

Royal priesthood service (gospel, ministry, etc.) involves the use of spiritual abilities which are a gift of grace from God (Ephesians 4:7). No one person should dominate in the service of an Assembly (3 John v.9). Every believer has received a spiritual gift (1 Corinthians 12:7), and these gifts differ between people in type and degree (1 Corinthians 12:4-6). These abilities are developed through use (1 Timothy 4:14); as these abilities become evident, they may be recognized and acknowledged by the overseers in the assembly so that the brother or sister is designated for particular service (1 Timothy 4:14).

A person can, over time, discover what their gift(s) are as follows:

1. by what they are good at;
2. by what they care about;
3. by what mature brothers and sisters say (1 Timothy 4:14);
4. by their circumstances which would indicate to which service the Lord is calling them.

Many of the gifts are identified in Romans 12:6-8; 1 Corinthians 12:4-11; Ephesians 4:7-13;1 Peter 4:10. They are to be used in harmony and to benefit others. They are not a substitute for the power of the Spirit in us, but are the channel for that power. their objective is:

· to prepare God's people for the works of service; and so
· to build up the Body of Christ until we all reach unity in the Faith and in the knowledge of the Son of God; and
· become mature, attaining to the whole measure of the fulness of Christ (Ephesians 4:12,13).

In the early days of the New Testament there were also miraculous gifts: speaking in tongues (foreign languages) and healing. These were given as evidence of the divine authority of the apostles (Mark 16:17; Hebrews 2:4; 2 Corinthians 12:12) (refer to Session 14). Now that we no longer have apostles, and we do have the completed New Testament Scriptures, these miraculous gifts no longer apply (1 Corinthians 13:8-10).

b) Music:

Singing has always been an important part of the service of God (e.g. Hebrews 2:12). Instrumental accompaniment was used in the Old Testament because it was a part of a physical service (animal offerings, incense, etc.). It is not mentioned in the New Testament as part of the spiritual service of the spiritual house of God today, and so it is not considered to be appropriate.

c) Money:

The service of God often requires money, which God allows His people to donate for this purpose. In the Old Testament they were required to give a 'tithe' (1/10). In the house of God today, however, no amount is specified; instead we are to give cheerfully (2 Corinthians 9:7). It is not as important how much we give as it is how much we have left (Mark 12:41-44). The more we give, the more God will give us (Luke 6:38). We are not to solicit money from those not in the house of God (3 John v.7) - collections are to be taken from the saints (1 Corinthians 16:1).

Giving money to someone is one way of having fellowship with that person, and associating yourself with that person (e.g. Philippians 1:5); so we must exercise care as to who and what we give money, to not violate our separation. Collections are usually made regularly in churches of God for (e.g.): general expenses (e.g. hall maintenance), Lord's service (e.g. supporting Lord's servants, outreach, campwork) (1 Corinthians 16:1,2) and those in need (Romans 12:13; 15:26).

d) Firstfruits:

Don't give the Lord 'what's left'; give the Lord His portion first (i.e. our money, our time, our abilities, our meditations on Christ) - firstfruits are first both in time and in quality (i.e. the best). In our service for God, we should be careful not to 'rob God' by keeping for ourselves the firstfruits that belong to Him (see Malachi 3:8-10).

REVIEW QUESTIONS

1. Who has a spiritual gift?
2. What are some of the spiritual gifts?
3. What is their purpose?
4. Why is instrumental music not used in the house of God?
5. What are the regular funds for which collections are taken in churches of God?
6. What is the main principle to remember in giving money to the Lord?

MEMORY VERSE

1 Peter 2:9 - "But you are a chosen people, a royal priesthood, a people belonging to God, that you may declare the praises of him who called you out of darkness into his wonderful light."

DISCUSSION QUESTIONS

1. How can you find out for what service in the assembly you are gifted?
2. Identify certain people in your assembly that you think have particular gifts (whether public or private). How do they exercise them for the good of others?
3. Parts I and II of the hymnbook 'Psalms, Hymns and Spiritual Songs' used by the Churches of God are intended for different usage. What is the distinction?
4. Should we give 1/10 of our income today?

ASSIGNMENT

Write out a short paper on the meaning of 1 Peter 4:11.

20

THE PEOPLE OF GOD

OBJECTIVES

1. To understand who the people of God are today. 2. To understand some of the doctrinal errors that the people of God must avoid.

ADVANCE READING

Read the following Scriptures and write a brief statement summarizing each one: 1. Titus 2:13,14; 2. 1 Peter 2:9,10; 3. 2 Corinthians 6:16-18; 4. 1 John 4:1; 5. 2 Corinthians 11:13-15

TOPIC OVERVIEW

a) A holy people:

God's desire is that disciples of the Lord Jesus Christ should be in churches of God and, together, form a holy people especially for Him (1 Peter 2:9). This was one of the purposes for which Christ died (Titus 2:14). Holiness is a requirement for those who are closely connected with God Himself (1 Peter 1:15,16). Holiness involves being separate from other things (sanctify = 'set apart') and being clean from defilement (sin; the world).

The 'people of God' refers to those in the house of God, not to all believers. It is important for the people of God to know the doctrine of the Lord and to know the doctrinal errors of some other churches and religions (1 John 4:1; 2 Corinthians 11:13-15; Matthew 7:15-23).

b) Frequently encountered denominations and religious groups:

(The following information is supplied in alphabetical order; it has been derived from a variety of sources and is correct to the best of our knowledge):

- **ALLIANCE:** Salvation is obtainable through a belief in Christ and works, and can be lost through not continuing in the disciple pathway. Miracles, tongues and healings have a place in our Christian living today. Scripture is not necessarily inerrant and not all parts are relevant.
- **ANGLICAN**: Christening brings a baby into the family of God and the kingdom of heaven. This early passive step is confirmed by the person at about 12 years of age following which the person is made a member of the Anglican church. Salvation can only be assured when the whole of life's works are tallied up and the final reward is given. Scripture is not necessarily inerrant and all parts are not relevant.
- **BAPTIST**: Salvation is through faith apart from works and baptism is a church sacrament. The Baptist church is really a loose conglomerate of hundreds of different groups of churches, each group having differing beliefs from the others. Some believe that the Bible, though correct in all matters concerning salvation, could be in error in other matters.
- **CHRISTADELPHIAN**: They deny the deity and eternal Sonship of Christ, the personality of both the Holy Spirit and Satan, the existence of hell, but believe you need to be saved through believing in Christ's death and having your sins washed away through baptism. Part of their approach is to infiltrate gospel meetings and argue with the speaker and with those who have been invited to attend.

- **CHRISTIAN REFORM**: Salvation is through faith plus works; salvation may be lost; baptism is not taught. One will not know whether he is saved until the end

- **CHRISTIAN SCIENCE**: They propagate the teachings of Mary Baker Eddy, teaching that death and disease are not real, but are figments of the imagination.

- **EXCLUSIVE BRETHREN**: They are a closely knit fellowship of assemblies numbering over half a million believers who hold all the proper doctrines of deity and scriptural inerrance. They believe, however, that God's house is in ruins; overseers do not exist today. Household baptism -the immersion of infants and young children - is held by some of them, and is supposed to bring them into a special relationship with God. They believe that once a person has come to a knowledge of what they believe and rejects it that he is not saved and never was, though he may have been once with them.

- **FULL GOSPEL**: 'Full' or 'Foursquare' gospel churches believe in the 'charismatic' gifts of tongues and healings and see these as a necessary manifestation of the Spirit to prove one's salvation. Being 'baptized by the Spirit' (not a scriptural term) is seen as something akin to being 'slain in the Spirit', after which one is filled with the Spirit, which is distinct from the Spirit's working at salvation.

- **JEHOVAH'S WITNESS**: They deny the eternal Sonship and Deity of the Lord Jesus Christ, the personality of the Holy Spirit and Satan, and the existence of hell. No one can know that he is saved until the last day; Christ has already returned to earth and we are already living in the tribulation period. Only Jehovah's witnesses will be saved, they must work to be saved, and everyone will have a second chance to become a Jehovah's witness after resurrection. Others will be annihilated. No person will ever live in heaven or is alive there now. Christ is simply an excelling God-pleasing angel.

- **JUDAISM:** Religious Jews believe that there is one God, Jehovah; they deny the existence of a Son of God and the person of the Holy Spirit, either of whom could be equal to Jehovah. The New Testament is therefore spurious, Christ is not the Messiah, and salvation must come through keeping the commandments of the law and its ramifications as presented through their various rabbis and teachers.

- **LUTHERAN:** Salvation is by faith apart from works, but it is possible to be saved by proxy, i.e. a child is saved through immersion in water upon the confession of its parent on its behalf that it believes.
- **METHODISM:** They believe that salvation is through faith plus works; they annul certain parts of Scripture; and they believe in the possibility of being saved and lost again.
- **MORMONISM:** They deny Christ's eternal Sonship and deity, the existence of hell, and the personality of Satan and the Holy Spirit. They deny the inerrance of Scripture, replacing it with the Book of Mormon and other books equal to it in authority. They believe that Christ visited North America in the flesh, as did John the Baptist, who appeared to Joseph Smith, their founder, repealing the Melchizedek priesthood and reinstating the Aaronic order which is centred on Mormonism. Every person, like Christ, has a heavenly spirit mother and father and can, through a good life, elevate himself to becoming one of the godhead.
- **MUSLIM:** There is no god but Allah, and Mohammed is his prophet. Christ was a good man, similar to the wise gurus of Islam, but was not deity nor God's eternal Son. Allah's book is the Koran, which teaches that a man must continue to pray and work for salvation.
- **NAZARENE:** See 'Full Gospel' and 'Pentecostal' with whom they share many beliefs.
- **OPEN BRETHREN:** A loose term which covers a wide range of unconnected fellowships of believers. They all believe in the complete autonomy of churches. The very 'open' groups receive any professing Christian to the table for the breaking of the bread; the 'tight' companies receive only on letter of commendation from their own group of churches. The looser groups have recently accepted the idea of pastors as main speakers in their groups and some practise charismatics (speaking in tongues and miraculous healing).
- **PENTECOSTAL:** A loose term (covering a wide range of charismatic

assemblies (see 'Full Gospel' above)). Falling away from salvation, a wide variety of entertainment in services, and selective Scripture acceptance characterize their meetings. Baptism and the Remembrance are generally not practised.

- **PRESBYTERIAN**: They preach salvation by works; they do not generally baptize, nor believe in the inerrancy of Scripture.
- **ROMAN CATHOLIC**: They deny salvation through faith apart from works, which accords the status of deity to humans (e.g. Mary), adds the writings of the Catholic church to the inspired Word of God, which accords infallibility to humans, and which sells indulgences and forgiveness of sin. It forbids certain to marry and to partake of some foods on certain days (this is waning somewhat).
- **SALVATION ARMY**: A philanthropic institution run along military lines whose main aim is to help people spiritually and temporally. They deny the relevance of certain parts of Scripture, forbidding baptism and the Remembrance. They believe in the falling-away doctrine.
- **SEVENTH DAY ADVENTIST**: This group demands the keeping of the Jewish sabbath, the refraining from certain foods and keeping of certain holidays as necessary for salvation. They are a very philanthropic group who deny the inerrancy of Scripture and tend to confuse the old and new dispensations.
- **SPIRITIST (SPIRITUALIST):** They believe in communication between the living and the dead through the offices of a medium. Many of their meetings are seances. They believe the Holy Spirit to be a means of such communication and see the Lord Jesus as chief medium.
- **UNITARIAN**: They deny the deity and Sonship of Christ and deny salvation through faith. They accept the Jewish concept of God but add the possibility of being a part of deity through a unity with nature and one's fellow man.
- **UNITED CHURCH**: A union of Methodist and one or two other churches; they deny the inspiration of parts of the Bible and do not accept the teaching of salvation through faith. Sermons deal largely with good living, and political and temporal themes.

- **WITNESS LEE**: They deny the bodily resurrection of Christ; they indoc-
  trinate their members through communal living practices, and make
  obedience to Scripture secondary to 'listening to the god within oneself.'

c) Erroneous beliefs:

The above-mentioned groups have many erroneous beliefs in common. The
doctrines of Scripture in which there is the most frequent error are as follows:

[1] The deity and eternal Sonship of Christ

Many groups believe Jesus of Nazareth was a good man or a notable prophet,
but not the eternal Son of God. They might base this on Hebrews 1:5,6 which
they interpret to mean that Jesus was created by God. However, see verse 8 of
the same chapter in which God refers to His Son as 'God'. See also Philippians
2:6; John 1:1,2 and Session 12.

[2] The inerrancy of Scripture

Many groups believe that only part of the Bible is totally reliable and applicable
today. See 2 Timothy 3:16,17; Romans 15:4 and Session 5.

[3] Salvation by faith in Christ alone

- not by works (e.g. a good life, keeping the law). This is sometimes based
  on James 2:14; however works in this Scripture are as the proof of the
  faith, not in addition to it. See Ephesians 2:8,9; Galatians 2:16 and Session
  2;
- not by baptism (i.e. baptismal regeneration). This is sometimes based
  on Mark 16:16 which, as verse 17 shows, was just for the apostolic period.
  See 1 Peter 3:20; Matthew 28:19 (it was disciples who were to be baptized)
  and Session 3.

[4] Personality of the Holy Spirit

Some groups believe that this just refers to the 'influence' of God. However, see John 14:23; Ephesians 4:30 and Session 13.

[5] Eternal security

Many groups believe in the 'falling away' doctrine - i.e. that a person can lose their eternal salvation. Some base it on Hebrews 6:4-6, and 10:26-31; however, all of these Scriptures refer to the loss of fellowship with God and the loss of the reward for service done. For eternal security, see John 10:28,29 and Session 2.

[6] Believers' baptism

Some groups do not practise this, or they believe it is optional. Some sprinkle infants, rather than immersing disciples (see Acts 8:39 for an instance of immersion). Some believe in baptism of whole households (based on Acts 16:33; however verses 32 and 34 show that the whole household heard the gospel and believed it). See Matthew 28:19; Acts 2:42; Acts 10:48 and Session 3.

[7] Miraculous gifts

Some groups believe that miraculous healing and speaking in tongues is applicable today, based on the fact that they occurred in the apostolic period. However, see 1 Corinthians 13:8, James 5:15 and Session 14.

[8] Rule by united elders

Some groups believe in rule by elders in each local church; others do not, sometimes on the basis that there are no longer apostles to appoint them (however Paul told Titus, as an elder, to appoint other elders - Titus 1:5). See

1 Timothy 3:1-7,15; Acts 20:28 and Session 21.

REVIEW QUESTIONS

1. Who are the people of God today?
2. What is the primary characteristic of God's people?
3. What are the common doctrinal errors that are to be avoided?

MEMORY VERSE

Titus 2:13,14 - "... we wait for the blessed hope - the glorious appearing of our great God and Saviour, Jesus Christ, who gave himself for us to redeem us from all wickedness to purify for himself a people that are his very own, eager to do what is good."

DISCUSSION QUESTIONS

Following are questions that are sometimes raised about the doctrines and practices of the churches of God today. From the scriptures referred to, how would you answer these?

1. "Any lack of numbers, fruitbearing and church growth must indicate that the doctrine is not correct" (1 Kings 18:19-22; Psalm 73; Jude 3; Revelation 2,3).
2. "Sisters have an 'inferior' place in the churches." (1 Corinthians 14:34,35; Colossians 3:18; 1 Peter 3:1-7; 1 Timothy 2:8-15).
3. "We shouldn't have to keep separate from other churches" (i.e. 'ecclesiastical separation'). (Matthew 7:17-23; Matthew 18:17,18; Romans 16:17,18; 1 Corinthians 5:9-11; 2 Thessalonians 3:6,14,15; 2 Timothy 3:5; Titus 3:10,11; 2 John 9-11; 2 Corinthians 6:14).
4. "Marriage in the Lord: What does it mean?" (1 Corinthians 7:39; Romans 16:2; 1 Corinthians 4:17; 1 Corinthians 9:1; Ephesians 2:21; 1 Corinthians 11:11; Philippians 1:14; 4:1,2; Colossians 4:7).

5. "Many statements made by those who minister in our meetings are just too vague or abstract to be understood by most people listening; for example: 'the dispensation of grace'; 'the day of the Lord'; 'baptismal regeneration'; 'holy priesthood service'; 'the knowledge of the truth.'" Make a list of all such terms that you can think of and write down a clear definition.

6. There is sometimes confusion about the distinction between 'fellowship' and 'the Fellowship', 'truth' and 'the Truth', 'faith' and 'the Faith'. Define them on the basis of Colossians 1:23; Jude 3; Acts 6:7; 14:22; 1 Timothy 6:12; 1 Timothy 1:19; 2 Timothy 3:8; 1 Timothy 4:6; Acts 16:5; also 1 Timothy 2:4; 3:15; 2 Timothy 3:17; Titus 1:1; Hebrews 10:26; Acts 2:42; 1 Corinthians 1:9.

7. How can we learn the difference between what we hold that is based on Scripture and what we hold that is built on tradition or inhibition? (e.g. why do men stand to pray?).

8. On what scriptural basis do we do the following: [a] say a united 'Amen' at the end of an assembly prayer? [b] address God as 'the God and Father of our Lord Jesus Christ'? [c] not allow women to pray when men are present? [d] sing a hymn after partaking of the cup in the Remembrance? [e] only allow part of the hymn book to be used in the Remembrance? [f] not allow Sunday school to be held before the Remembrance?

ASSIGNMENT

Select one or more of the other churches or denominations listed in this session, with which you have had some contact, and find out more about their key doctrines and why they believe them. Show whether those doctrines are scriptural or not.

21

THE KINGDOM OF GOD

OBJECTIVES

1. To understand what the kingdom of God is today. 2. To understand the roles of overseers, deacons and saints in the churches of God, in the kingdom of God.

ADVANCE READING

Read the following Scriptures and write a brief summary of the main point of each one: 1. Exodus 19:6; 2. Judges 21:25; 3. Luke 12:32; 4. Acts 1:3; 5. Philippians 1:1; 6. 1 Timothy 3:1-15; 7. Acts 15:1-35; 8. 1 Corinthians 11:3

TOPIC OVERVIEW

(a) What is the kingdom of God?

The kingdom of God comprises saints, some of whom are deacons, and some are overseers (also called bishops, elders, the presbytery).

(b) Overseers:

Overseers are men who, collectively, have the responsibility under God for the rule and leadership in the churches of God; it is a 'noble task' (1 Timothy 3:1). They were originally appointed by the apostles (Acts 14:23), or under the apostles' direction (Titus 1:5). Overseers are made overseers by the Holy Spirit (Acts 20:28). 1 Timothy 3:1-7 gives their qualifications:

- above reproach;
- husband of just one wife;
- temperate, self-controlled, respectable;
- hospitable;
- able to teach;
- not given to much wine;
- not violent, but gentle;
- not quarrelsome;
- not a lover of money;
- a good manager of his own family, with obedient children;
- not a recent convert; and
- has a good reputation with outsiders.

Overseers are compared to shepherds who have the care of their flock (1 Peter 5:1-5):

- they are to feed the sheep (teach the saints) (John 21:15-17);
- they are to tend the sheep (care for the saints);
- they are under the Lord Jesus, who is the Chief Shepherd (1 Peter 5:4);
- they have to give account for those under their care (Hebrews 13:17).

Overseers make decisions collectively, not as individuals. This ensures that no one individual has too much influence. Reaching agreement with each other is an indication that they know the mind of the Lord on a particular matter (Acts 15:25,28). This collective action takes place at three levels:

1. **local** – the overseers of a church of God;
2. **district or country** – the overseers of all the churches of God in that area;
3. **worldwide** – the overseers of all districts in the Fellowship of Churches of God.

This unity of brothers together is a delight to the Lord (Psalm 133:1) and requires overseers to submit themselves to one another.

The saints in the assembly (including individual overseers) are told in Hebrews 13 how they are to act toward their overseers: think of them (such as, in prayer), imitate them (verse 7), obey and submit to them (verse 17) and communicate with them (verse 24).

The overseers are over the saints in terms of their authority, but are instructed to live among the saints; that is, they are to keep in touch with them, not stay aloof and not 'lord' their authority over them. They are to be 'role models' (see 1 Thessalonians 5:12; 1 Peter 5:1,2).

(c) Deacons:

Deacons are men who have been appointed, by the overseers of their assembly, for certain types of service. The word deacon means servant, and it is used of Christ. All saints (brothers and sisters) can serve in the assembly (for example, Phoebe in Romans 16:1,2); but deacons are appointed to their service permanently. Their qualifications are given in 1 Timothy 3:8-13:

- worthy of respect;
- sincere;
- not indulging in much wine;
- not pursuing dishonest gain;
- solid in the Faith (doctrine);
- proven;
- husband of just one wife; and

· manages his family well.

These qualifications are similar to those of overseers (above). They work in the assembly together with the overseers and their work is worthy of high honour (1 Timothy 3:13).

(d) Assembly action

Although overseers provide the leadership, certain decisions require the united action of the whole Assembly (such as the addition and excommunication of saints). The Assembly displays its assent to the action by together saying 'amen', which means 'so be it.' (For example: Nehemiah 5:13). Saints also should audibly say Amen at the end of an Assembly prayer or thanksgiving to indicate that it comes from the whole Assembly (1 Corinthians 14:16).

(e) 'Lord's servants':

There is no 'one man ministry' in churches of God. There is no minister or clergy. (The word 'reverend' only occurs once, in Psalm 111:9 (RV), and there it is not a title but a description of the name of God.) However, the Lord has provided for certain brothers to be called to work for Him on a full-time basis and to be financially supported by the saints (1 Corinthians 9:13,14; 1 Corinthians 16:1-3; Philippians 4: 15-17).

(f) The role of women ('sisters'):

Women are not to take the lead. It is the men's role to minister the Word of God to the assembly and to pray and give thanks on behalf of the assembly. The women are to remain silent (1 Timothy 2:11,12). They are to cover their hair in assembly gatherings to show their subjection to the men in this service (1 Corinthians 11:10). The role of women is based on the principle of headship (1 Corinthians 11:3). They can fully participate audibly in private service. The man and the woman are not independent of each other in the Lord (1

Corinthians 11:11).

REVIEW QUESTIONS

1. When did God introduce the concept of rule within a kingdom?
2. Who constituted the kingdom of God in Old Testament times?
3. Who constitute the kingdom of God today?
4. What are the roles in a church of God, according to Philippians 1:1?
5. What are the responsibilities of overseers?
6. How do overseers make decisions?
7. How should the saints act towards their overseers?
8. What are the responsibilities of deacons?
9. When should the assembly say Amen, and what does it mean?
10. What is women's role in the assembly?

MEMORY VERSE

Acts 20:28 - 'Keep watch over yourselves and all the flock of which the Holy Spirit has made you overseers. Be shepherds of the church of God, which He bought with His own blood.'

DISCUSSION QUESTIONS

1. What qualifications of deacons are similar to those of overseers, according to 1 Timothy 3?
2. What is the main lesson of the conference of elders in Acts 15?
3. What districts of churches of God are identified in 1 Peter 1, 2 Corinthians 8 and 9?
4. What should you do if you don't agree with a decision of your overseers?
5. How should sisters in the assembly participate in the Remembrance and prayer meetings?
6. Who are the overseers and deacons in your assembly?
7. Who are the full-time Lord's Servants in the Fellowship at present, and

which country do they live in?

ASSIGNMENT

Make a list of what you think are the matters facing overseers and deacons in your assembly and district at present.

22

FELLOWSHIP AND SEPARATION

OBJECTIVES

1. To understand the importance to God of unity among things that are the same, and separation from those that are opposed to Him. 2. To get practical help on how to live separated lives as disciples in the world.

ADVANCE READING

Read the following Scriptures and write a brief statement summarizing each one: 1. Ephesians 5:11; 2. 1 John 1:7; 3. 1 John 2:15,16 4. 2 Thessalonians 3:6,14,15 5. Leviticus 10:10

TOPIC OVERVIEW

a) The divine principle of light and darkness

God is light (1 John 1:5); Satan controls the darkness (Luke 22:53). At the creation, God first divided the light from the darkness since they cannot co-exist. At our salvation, we were turned "from darkness to light" (Acts 26:18). God thus joined things that were the same, and separates things that are different. God now calls us to "have no fellowship with the unfruitful works of darkness" (Ephesians 5:11 RV) for "what communion has light with darkness?" (2 Corinthians 6:14 NKJV). "If we walk in the light, as he is in the light, we have fellowship with one another" (1 John 1:7). This requires wisdom, because Satan tries to deceive us by fashioning himself into an angel of light (2 Corinthians 11:14 RV).

b) The need for separation:

God taught Israel in the Old Testament to "put difference between the holy and the common, between the clean and the unclean" (Leviticus 10:10 RV). They were to be holy, because God was holy (Leviticus 11:45) so that they could engage in service for God. They were also to be clean in their personal lives. At the time of the Passover in Egypt, God told them that He put a difference between the Egyptians and Israel (Exodus 11:7). Disciples of the Lord Jesus today are also called to be a) **separate from** anything that is not of God - e.g. things in the world, unscriptural churches and associations, ungodly people, and b) **separate to** what is of God - to have fellowship with God the Father, and His Son, and other people who are joined together for the same purpose – 'saints'.

c) Separation from the world:

"Do not love the world or anything in the world. If anyone loves the world, the love of the Father is not in him. For everything in the world - the cravings of sinful man, the lust of his eyes and the boasting of what he has and does - comes not from the Father but from the world" (1 John 2:15,16). Some examples of things in the world:

- **politics** (including supporting political parties) and voting - we are subject to those in authority (Romans 13:1) and should pray for them (1 Timothy 2:2), but it is not our responsibility to use the political process (Philippians 3:20; I Corinthians 5:12);

- **military service** - we are not to join the armed forces to engage in combat or carry arms (John 18:36);
- **entertainment** - a lot of entertainment in the world appeals to the flesh, and is harmful to our spiritual lives (Galatians 5:17);
- **gambling** - we are not to have a love for money (1 Timothy 6:10); money is given to us, as stewards, by God to use wisely and generously (Luke 6:38);
- **extra-marital sexual activity** - fornication, adultery, incest, homosexuality, etc. are all serious moral sins with God (1 Corinthians 6:18-20).

Disciples are not given a complete list in Scripture of do's and dont's; instead they are given some criteria for assessing any activity - such as:

- is it according to the Word of God? (Psalm 119:105);
- is it to the glory of God, since our bodies are temples of God? (1 Corinthians 10:31; 2 Corinthians 6:7-19);
- how will it affect my love for the Lord? (1 John 2:15);
- how will it affect others? (1 Corinthians 8:13; 10:32);
- is there a relevant example from the Lord's life? (1 Peter 2:21);
- how will it affect the testimony of the Lord's people? (1 Peter 2:9);
- is it making good use of our time? (Ephesians 5:15-17);
- is there a better alternative? (Luke 10:42).

As we follow our conscience (the leading of the Spirit), it will grow stronger through use, to be able to differentiate between what is good and what is not (Hebrews 5:14). Christ referred to his disciples as being in the world, but not of it (John 17:15,16).

d) Separation from other believers:

All believers have a common life in Christ (Galatians 3:28) but not all believers know about, or are obedient to, the place where God wants all believers to be - the house of God. That place has clear boundaries and identity; there is an inside and outside (1 Corinthians 5:12,13). The house of God is the place of God's choosing for all collective worship and service. Any other gathering together or association which takes its place is contrary to that. Therefore, the 'churches (ecclesia = called out together to ...) of God' must be separate from other denominations. Christ prayed that His disciples might "all be one" (John 17:21), sanctified "in the truth" (John 17:17). The truth of God is available to all (1 Timothy 2:4) and is the only basis on which disciples should be joined together for divine service (1 Timothy 3:15). The price of the truth has always been separation; for example:

- Paul had to separate from Judaism when he learned the truth of Christ; later he said that if he were to go back and support Judaism, he would be a transgressor (Galatians 2:18);
- Paul, at Ephesus (Acts 19:9), separated those willing to learn;
- Martin Luther had to leave the Catholic church when he learned the truth of justification by faith, because they would not accept it;
- the Ana-baptists had to leave the established churches because they practised the baptism of believers;
- Christian brethren in the early 19th century had to leave the national churches when they discovered the truths of the Church the Body of Christ, the Remembrance, etc.

e) Separation from believers in churches of God:

God even requires disciples in churches of God to separate themselves from other disciples in churches of God who are:

- teaching wrong doctrine (Titus 1:10,11);
- sinning wilfully (2 Thessalonians 3:6; 1 Corinthians 5:9-11);
- disregarding the teaching and guidance of the leaders (2 Thessalonians 3:14,15);
- trouble-makers (Titus 3:10).

When someone is put away from a church of God, they are under the judgement of the Lord that they might be brought to repentance and restoration (1 Corinthians 5:3-5). By associating with them as though they were still in the house of God we could frustrate God's purpose in their lives (2 Timothy 2:25).

f) Separation vs. outreach:

Disciples are told not to love the world (1 John 2:15) but we are told that God did love the world (John 3:16). This is not a contradiction, of course – God's love was for the people that He might save them out of the world. One of the reasons that believers are left in the world is to reach out that others might be saved. Our association with unbelievers, therefore, should not be for fellowship (sharing) with them (Ephesians 5:11; 2 Timothy 3:1-5) but should be for winning them for Christ (1 Corinthians 9:19-23). We have to assess our own motives, therefore, in what we do with unbelievers.

REVIEW QUESTIONS

1. What is God's divine principle of separation? What is an illustration of it?
2. Between what things were Israel instructed in the Old Testament to put a distinction?
3. What are some of the things in the world from which disciples should be separate?
4. What are eight criteria for assessing a particular activity?
5. Complete this sentence: "We are ... the world, but not ... it."
6. Why do disciples have to be separate from some other believers?
7. Give some examples of where people had to separate in order to practise the truth of God that they had learned.
8. From what kinds of people within churches of God should we also keep separate?
9. How should we act towards someone put away from a church of God?

MEMORY VERSE

1 John 2:15,16 - "Do not love the world, or anything in the world. If anyone loves the world, the love of the Father is not in him. For everything in the world - the cravings of sinful man, the lust of his eyes and the boasting of what he has and does - comes not from the Father but from the world."

DISCUSSION QUESTIONS

1. What is meant in 1 John 1:3-7 by our fellowship with the Father, the Son and each other?
2. How can you explain to other believers why you are restricted in the fellowship you can have with them?
3. Choose one or two types of your free-time activities, and apply the criteria set out in the Topic Overview above, to decide how appropriate they are.
4. Give an example of each of the following (1 John 2:16 RV): [a] 'the lust of the flesh' [b] 'the lust of the eyes' [c] 'the vain-glory of life.'
5. In what sense do the churches of God together form a 'fellowship'? (1 Corinthians 1:9).
6. What is the harm in attending churches other than the church of God?
7. Why can associating with someone excommunicated from a church of God create problems? How should you treat them?

ASSIGNMENT

During the coming week, make a note of all the situations where it would be easy for you to break your separation from the world to the things of God.

23

THE HISTORY OF THE FELLOWSHIP

OBJECTIVES:

1. To understand that throughout history God has desired a single dwelling place among people. 2. To appreciate how God revived His house about 100 years ago by establishing the present churches of God.

ADVANCE READING

No reading for this session.

TOPIC OVERVIEW

a) God's people in the Old Testament:

God first showed Jacob at Bethel (Beth-el = 'house of God') the idea of a house of God (Genesis 18). God could not have a house during the time of Genesis, because it required a collective people (Genesis is a book about individuals).God called the nation of Israel out of Egypt to be His people (Exodus 5:1) and a priesthood (Exodus 19:6). They were referred to as 'the church in the wilderness' (Acts 7:38 RV). When He had made a covenant with them, He told them to 'make me a sanctuary that I may dwell among them' (Exodus 25:8 RV). This first house of God was a tent ('tabernacle'); it was later replaced by a temple that was built by Solomon in Jerusalem in times when Israel reached its peak.

After that time, however, there was a steady decline, which resulted in the people being taken captive to Babylon and the house of God being destroyed. During the seventy years' captivity, the people of God were in the wrong place and the house of God was in ruins. Only a remnant (a small fraction) of the people ever returned and the restoration of the nation was accomplished in stages. The house of God had to be rebuilt (by Ezra and then rebuilt by Herod) and its glory was a far cry from Solomon's temple. But God again had a people back in the land and His house was again functioning.When Christ came, He announced the rejection of Israel (Luke 13:35) and the transfer of the kingdom to His disciples (Matthew 21:43; Luke 12:32). Their house was left desolate (Matthew 23:38) and a new spiritual house of God substituted (1 Peter 2:5).

This reached its peak during the time of the apostles as churches of God were planted throughout parts of the Roman Empire. But, just as in Old Testament times, there was decline for many years, followed by a gradual restoration to the original New Testament pattern. During this dispensation of time (almost 2000 years long now) God has not changed His arrangement, but His house has not been in existence for most of this period.

b) God's people in the New Testament:

The physical temple was replaced as the house of God by a spiritual house; people themselves became indwelt by God as a temple (1 Peter 2:5; 1 Corinthians 3:16).It consisted of churches of God that were 'planted' in various cities and countries during the first century A.D. (Acts 8:1; 9:31). Paul predicted a decline of the truth (Acts 20:29,30; 2 Timothy 4:3,4) and John tells us that churches can cease to exist (Revelation 2:5). This happened towards the end of the first century as men added to and took away from the Lord's teaching to His disciples. They preserved the Bible, but not its teaching of the church of God.

c) The Decline (about AD 100 to 1500)

Apostasy - that is a falling away from the true teaching (2 Timothy 4:3,4) - happened progressively in the centuries that followed the completion of the Scriptures. The main problem was that human tradition gradually replaced scriptural doctrine (Matthew 15:2,3; Colossians 2:8).What emerged was the all-powerful Roman Catholic church which held certain basic doctrines which were contrary to the Scriptures, such as:

1. an infallible Pope, who was a go-between between man and God;
2. a hierarchy of clergy (specialists), distinct from the laity (church members);
3. 'Baptismal regeneration' - baptism of infants, followed by confirmation when the age of understanding was reached, for the purpose of obtaining salvation. This salvation had to be maintained by repeated confessions to a priest and payment of money;
4. celebration of the Mass, performed by the clergy frequently in Latin, instead of the simple Remembrance;
5. involvement in politics and accumulation of enormous wealth;
6. worship of relics, adornment of buildings, etc.

Despite this increasing departure from the apostles' doctrine, the Bible was preserved throughout the years. Also history records many faithful individuals who held to the truth, often being martyred for it.

d) The Reformation (about AD 1500)

JOHN WYCLIFFE (born 1324) translated the Bible into English for the common people to be able to read it. Printing presses made the Bible available to those who previously would not have seen one.

MARTIN LUTHER (1483 - 1546) was a German academic who, as a result of Bible study in his 30s became convinced of sin and need for a Saviour and rediscovered the scriptural principle of justification by faith, not works (Romans 1:17; 5:1) - the unique doctrine of Christianity. He began to preach this and other scriptural doctrines in the hope of reforming the Catholic church from within, opposing the incorrect teachings of the Catholic church which had held religious sway for about 1,400 years. After long and bitter antagonism, which focused on the authority of Scripture versus the authority of the Pope, he found it necessary to leave the Roman Catholic Church. But he, along with other reformers of his time, helped change the face of religion.

Luther had realized the scriptural principle of the need to separate from those who do not hold the truth in order to be able to practise it (2 Corinthians 6:14-18; 2 Timothy 2:19-21). The truths of God, so long hidden by man's tradition, were beginning to be brought to light by the Spirit of God working in men who studied their Bibles. From Luther, Calvin, Wesley, there began a number of Protestant evangelical churches (such as the Presbyterian, Methodist, and Baptist) over a number of years. However these churches tended to keep many of the old traditions, such as nationalism, mixed congregations (both saved and unsaved members), one-man ministry ('clerisy'). They had not managed to recover all the Truth, but had completed the first stage.

e) The Brethren Movement (about 1830)

About 1827 (around the time the Pentecostal movement began also), a number of spiritual believers in Dublin, Ireland and Plymouth, England began to be concerned about the condition of these institutional churches. They were especially unhappy about:

1. one-man ministry (they realized the Remembrance should be participated in equally by all disciples);
2. (mixed congregations (believers should not worship with unbelievers); and

3. the disunity among believers with the numerous denominations ('sects') that existed.

The leaders of this movement were Mr. Groves and Mr. Darby in Dublin, Ireland and Mr. Newton in Plymouth (thus the name 'Plymouth Brethren'). It became known as the Christian Brethren Movement. They began to teach separation from unbelievers for the Remembrance, and the error of one man ministry ('clerisy'). They emphasized the Remembrance meeting and gathered for it based only on salvation – 'the common life in Christ'. The Lord's table (at the Remembrance) was sometimes referred to as the Father's table so that all children of God (that is, believers) could participate. It was not necessary for those believers to leave the other churches.

The major difficulty, which became apparent when problems arose, was they deliberately had no basic doctrine of organization. Thus leadership tended to come from influential men in individual assemblies and there developed a pronounced lack of uniformity among them. They had no concept at this point of a church of God being any different from the Church the Body of Christ, and they freely mingled with the denominations. They had no constitution, no doctrine, no organization based on Scripture. However key men in various cities took the leadership in putting into practice what they were learning.

f) The 'Exclusive Brethren' (about 1850):

About 1845 this problem came to a head. Mr. Groves and Mr. Newton realized that formal leadership was necessary and that the scriptural method was for overseers to be recognized in each new church. Mr. Darby felt that recognized overseers could only be done by the original New Testament apostles and felt that the solution was to have a strong central assembly which could deal with disputes affecting the other assemblies. It was a debate between decentralization and centralization; unfortunately they missed the scriptural principle of a united oversight in a fellowship of churches.

The result of this was that Mr. Darby and a group of about 60 others split off and became known as the 'Exclusive' Brethren (its centre was Park Avenue assembly in London, England). They believed that the 'church of God' only existed in New Testament times, is now in ruins and so should not be restored. Organization can therefore be based on convenience rather than New Testament examples and principles. The 'exclusive movement' has been characterized by single dominant personalities.

The Open Brethren continued to be organized in a very loose way. They realized that basing fellowship only on salvation created some difficulties and so added the condition that the believers be 'sound in faith' and 'godly in life', although these terms were undefined. They de-emphasized doctrinal differences and freely permitted a brother to preach or worship in another church and then do the same with them. That is, they continued to have fellowship with the denominations they had left behind. They granted 'occasional fellowship' (such as while on holiday) - that is, a believer could visit them temporarily, keep the breaking of the bread, and then leave, without the need to be 'added' or 'commended'. Each assembly was autonomous; assembly A would have fellowship with assembly B but not with assembly C - yet assembly B would have fellowship with assembly C.

g) The Separation of the Churches of God (1892-94)

The Brethren movement was a great step forward in the separation of believers from the national churches, with their clerisy. But it failed to go far enough in realizing the complete unity of the Fellowship of the Lord Jesus (1 Corinthians 1:9). One of the most important writings at this time was a pamphlet called 'The Church, and the Churches of God - A Suggestive Outline of Truth' written by Frederick Arthur Banks, who was in his early twenties. The late 1880s saw considerable concern about this whole matter and was the reason for the magazine Needed Truth being started in 1888. Here is a brief summary of some of the issues that they were concerned about:

1. No separation from the denominations;
2. All believers, regardless of doctrinal belief, were permitted to have fellowship in the breaking of the bread;
3. Gathering together was based only on salvation, or, in some cases, baptism, rather than God's calling into a defined Fellowship;
4. Relationship between assemblies was based either on local preference (Open Brethren) or a central authority (Exclusives), rather than a united oversight, etc. which met together;
5. Association was only for the breaking of the bread, etc; rather than constituting the house of God (where God could be served) and the kingdom of God (where God's government could be exercised);
6. Various assemblies, with various doctrines, existing in one city, rather than there being a single united church of God in the city even though consisting of different companies;
7. Assemblies acted autonomously rather than in fellowship with the others and had a wide variety of practices;
8. Assemblies consisted only of those who happened to come together at any time rather than being called together as saints and added into a Fellowship of which Christ is Lord.

This was a time of great difficulty and searching of heart. Many wanted to stay in the Open Brethren movement and try to change the fundamental doctrines from within. But increasingly it became evident what the scriptural approach was:

1. a church of God should be constituted of those who have been 'called out' and 'added to the Lord' as a definite act (Acts 5:14);
2. the existence of the house of God depended, not on the number of people gathered today, but on the adherence to every doctrine of the Faith, regardless of how few people were involved (1 Timothy 3:15);
3. the formation of the house of God took place by living stones (believers) coming to Christ as their Lord (discipleship) to be built together (1 Peter 2);

4. if faithful ones are in the minority in an assembly where wrong doctrine persists, they should outpurge themselves (withdraw) from it (2 Timothy 2:19).

After teaching these newly-learned truths orally and in writing for some time, to little avail, and trying to resolve the matter at a special conference in 1891, it became apparent that a separation would be necessary (just as at the time of the Reformation and the Brethren Movement). The separation took place during 1892-4 and involved personal sacrifice by many who had to leave family, friends, etc. The new churches of God declared themselves and finally there was a mutually known Fellowship of about 100 assemblies, after a number of years of exercise.

h) The Vernal Trouble (1903)

Around 1903 trouble arose in Ayr, Scotland which resulted in 20 assemblies leaving the Fellowship, led by Mr. Frank Vernal. It had to do with lack of unity among overseers with respect to disciplining a brother in the assembly and then a lack of subjection to one another in attempting to restore unity. This sad episode stressed the importance of adhering to 1 Peter 5:5 in the working together of overseers and led to a clearer understanding of the spiritual procedure for resolving difficulties by taking them to the next higher level (e.g. districts).

(i) Today

Today there are churches of God in the Fellowship of the Son of God in all five continents - still functioning as the people of God, being ruled by a united oversight, and seeking to observe all things that the Lord has commanded us under one body of doctrine - and according to the principles and practice of the New Testament churches. At the time of publishing, there are almost 150 assemblies in 17 districts in 20 countries: Australia, Belgium, Canada, England, Ghana, India, Jamaica, Kenya, Liberia, Malawi, Mozambique,

Myanmar, Nigeria, Northern Ireland, Philippines, Scotland, Tanzania, U.S.A., Wales, Zimbabwe. (For further information, visit www.churchesofgod.info and refer to 'The Search for the Truth of God', published by Hayes Press).

REVIEW QUESTIONS

1. Where was the first house of God on earth?
2. Why did God reject the temple that had been built for Him?
3. With what was it replaced?
4. What is the definition of a 'temple of God'?
5. What must be the fundamental basis of the house of God, according to 1 Timothy 3:15?
6. What was the root cause for the decline of the house of God after New Testament times?
7. What's the basic difference between Open Brethren, Exclusive Brethren and the churches of God?
8. When did 'the Separation' take place, at which times churches of God, and the house of God, were re-established?

MEMORY VERSE

I Corinthians 1:9 (NKJV) - 'God is faithful, by whom you were called into the fellowship of his Son, Jesus Christ our Lord.

DISCUSSION QUESTIONS

1. How do you think most believers today decide to which church they should belong?
2. What are the two main publications of the churches of God and what are their respective purposes?
3. Discuss how the way that 'Open Brethren' and 'Exclusive Brethren' are organized can lead to problems.
4. How has history repeated itself in the re-establishment of the house of

God at the end of the nineteenth century, compared with Ezra's time?

5. If a church of Christians is doing all the same things as a church of God, does that automatically make it a church of God?

6. What lessons can we learn from the history of the house of God?

ASSIGNMENT

Find the location of a church of God in a country far away from yours, send them an email (via the assembly correspondent) identifying yourself, indicating that you are taking this course, and describe yourself and your Assembly.

SUGGESTED ANSWERS TO STUDY QUESTIONS

SESSION 1: DISCIPLESHIP

1. He spoke using illustrations and parables. He performed miracles to confirm His divine origin. His life was consistent with what He said. He quoted Old Testament Scriptures. He often used questions.
2. Read and study the Scriptures; get help from a more mature disciple; surrender your will to God (not your ability but your availability); pray in faith; look for opportunities (e.g. worship, disciple-making)
3. Whatever the every-day consequences of being a true disciple are - e.g. self-denial (time, money, relationships, certain types of entertainment), reproach etc.
4. All of these - firstly attitude, then a gradual increase in knowledge, which is put into practice.
5. Accepting Christ as a free gift is personal, it is invisible to others, the consequence is in the future and it is unconditional. Being a disciple, however, alters every-day life, it is apparent to others and is done in conjunction with others, and it is conditional on being obedient. The second requires the first.
6. The commendation of Christ and a future place of honour with Christ. Present fulfilment and meaning in life.
7. Selfishness, inconsistency, wrong ideas, wasting time, inability to witness, ignorance of Scripture, lack of spiritual influence on others, no difference from people in the world, living for own gratification.

8. By being taught and encouraged by other disciples, from the Scriptures.
9. Personal answer.

SESSION 2: THE REALITY OF SALVATION

1. The unilateral action of God whereby He deals kindly with us for our good, according to His own plans for us, despite the fact that we don't deserve any of it.

2. If God just condoned our sin, He would compromise His own righteousness and no longer be God; someone must pay the penalty. We cannot achieve God's standard of righteousness on our own; a single sin disqualifies us; so a means of salvation is necessary. Someone must bear the penalty of all our sin; his qualifications are that he must be (a) a member of the human race, so as to represent the human race, (b) be sinless himself so that he didn't himself need to be saved - only Christ met the qualifications. Once the salvation was obtained, it must be accepted voluntarily (by faith) - so that it wasn't forced on people.

3. To be given the status of totally righteous, as God is (as in a court of law, to be totally cleared of the accusation).

4. To be set aside from other things to be completely at God's disposal, and then to be cleansed to be useful to God - i.e. to be made 'holy'.

5. God only holds people accountable for what they know (Acts 17:30); however, even if they have not heard the gospel, everyone is accountable for believing that God created this earth because the evidence is sufficient (Romans 1:20). For those who have heard the gospel, they are accountable to believe it; rejecting Christ will result in eternal banishment from God in the lake of fire (Revelation 20:15).

6. Salvation occurs once, based on one act of faith, and is permanent. The Spirit seals you regardless of your life and service for Christ.

SESSION 3: WATER BAPTISM

1. Baptism is commanded for disciples; it is an individual decision; but for disciples who understand that they should be baptized, but fail to do so, it is disobedience.
2. Christ died to put away the power of sin; by being baptized we consciously choose to discontinue our previous life following our human nature and to make Him Lord of our lives.
3. Luke 8:2 – she followed Him after her salvation from Satanic power; John 19:25 – she was with the Lord at Calvary, at His death; Luke 23:55 – she was at His burial; John 20:1 – she was at His resurrection; Acts 1:13,14 – she was gathered with the other disciples who became the Church of God in Jerusalem.

SESSION 4: THE CONTENTS OF THE BIBLE

1. [a] Exodus [b] Psalms [c] Acts [d] epistles of John [e] 1 & 2 Samuel] [f] Hebrews [g] Revelation, Daniel, Isaiah, etc. [h] Ezra.
2. Christ, Noah, David, Joseph.
3. Unlikely to mean that the world does not have enough physical space for the books – more likely that the world would not accept more about the claims of Christ.
4. All do except #4; "remember the sabbath day...", which has been replaced by the Lord's Day, the first day of the week.
5. Rome (Acts 28) – west; Egypt (Genesis 12) – south (also Ethiopia – Acts 8);[Mesopotamia (Genesis 12) – east; Mt Ararat (Turkey) (Genesis 9) – north.
6. It is more objective and permanent; very few are privileged to have been eye-witnesses, but all can have access to the Scriptures.

SESSION 5: THE AUTHORITY OF SCRIPTURE

1. Potential explanations: a) Different but compatible accounts of the same event (Mark 10:46 does not say Bartimaeus was the only blind man) b) one account is more detailed; the other uses an approximation (this is a common practice) c) possible copyists error d) God has not clarified it (e.g. 2 Samuel 24:13 & 1 Chronicles 21:1).

2. The work of laying foundation doctrine was done by the apostles and prophets (Ephesians 2:20), who are no longer alive. Today God provides teachers to explain the doctrine (1 Corinthians 12:28). Some books explicitly preclude additions (Revelation 22:18; Proverbs 30:66). The unity of Scripture evidences its completion (Jude 3).

3. Some of the words that were spoken were clearly metaphors (e.g. Luke 13:32 - Herod was not a literal fox even though it is true that Jesus called him that; sometimes the Bible uses round numbers or approximations (as we do) Generally, we should take the statements literally unless they are fairly obviously just illustrations.

4. Disbelief in miracles, including the creation; denial of the reality of man's fall into sin, and thus the need for personal salvation; increased tolerance for immorality, believing Scripture to be only the author's opinion, or only culturally relevant; rejection of the teaching of subjection to authority.

SESSION 6: BIBLE READING AND STUDY

1. If I cannot properly answer questions about the doctrine; if I enjoy other reading more than the Word of God; if sin does not seem all that bad; if I'm quite content with my limited knowledge of God.

2. Regarding knowledge as an end in itself (2 Timothy 3:7); not permitting the Holy Spirit to guide you (1 Thessalonians 5:19); relying too heavily on commentaries; doing it only out of formality and ritual.

3. Natural ability is not enough - need the Holy Spirit and prayer; it has eternal value and gains God's approval.

4. Careful choice of participants - at the same general level of understanding, and compatible; competent but non-domineering leadership; prior individual study expected by all; participation by all encouraged but not forced; effective use of aids.

SESSION 7: PRAYER

1. Only the prayer of faith - for whoever comes to God must believe in Him (Hebrews 11:6). Normally prayer is a privilege restricted for the children of God - those who can call Him their Father (John 1:12). The Lord Jesus taught His disciples to pray 'our Father.'
2. Blocked fellowship with God (1 John 1:6) and unanswered prayer.
3. Prayer and alertness are two safeguards against succumbing to temptation.
4. Fasting is going without food. After the initial hunger wears off, it sharpens the mind and so permits more intensity in prayer.
5. Anywhere is acceptable, depending on the circumstances. But a quiet place alone is best (Matthew 6:6; Mark 1:35).
6. Victory depended on their persistence in prayer (Luke 18:1). Aaron and Hur supported Moses in his prayer - we can support others' prayers.
7. The spiritual condition of those in the assembly, especially those cold in heart; the effectiveness of gospel outreach; those in the assembly who are ill or in difficulty; the Lord's Servants, their work and their families; other assemblies, including weaker ones; overseers; camp work; etc.
8. Personal answer.
9. Personal answer.
10. No, although brevity is encouraged (Matthew 6:7). The fervency and the frequency are the important things.

SESSION 8: CHRISTLIKENESS

1. Previously he was personally ambitious (even in the things of God); afterwards he counted all those things as worth nothing; he "buffeted his body" constantly - i.e. he disciplined it to bring it into subjection. Everywhere he went, he preached and taught about Christ and the Kingdom of God.
2. The aim of a disciple of the Lord Jesus Christ is to be as like Christ as possible, while being in complete subjection to Him.
3. Personal answer.
4. It provides information on Christ's life in considerable detail; it describes the attributes of Christ which we are to imitate][it is totally authoritative and sufficient.
5. a) Control what you say, such as gossip (James 3:1-12); b) be sensitive to the needs of others, rather than always thinking of yourself (Romans 15:3 – "Christ also pleased not himself"); c) listen regularly to the Spirit's direction, through careful reading and meditation on Scripture and prayer (Luke 16:12); d) be totally honest - no white lies.

SESSION 9: VICTORY OVER SIN

1. Dead in sins; followed the ways of the world; subject to the spirit that now works in those who are disobedient; gratify the desires of the flesh; no one seeks God; worthless; deceitful; curse; murderous.
2. Adam's disobedience in the garden of Eden made the human race sinners, since all descendants of Adam have inherited a sinful nature. Christ's obedience in His life and death overcame the result of Adam's disobedience for all who believe on Him, so that they could become free of sin; Christ is the 'last Adam' (1 Corinthians 15:45) He finished what Adam started.
3. Personal answer.
4. No, our salvation is eternal and is assured; it is based on the completed work of Christ, not on our behaviour.

5. Go to them humbly, ask if it is true, and try to help them. If they should confess it to someone else, encourage them to do so (Galatians 6:1; Matthew 18:15-17).

6. Defeat in our struggle against the world (e.g. Achan); loss of joy in our Christian life, because of guilt (e.g. David - Psalm 51).

7. God made Him to be a sin-offering on Calvary - to be eligible, He Himself had to be sinless so that He didn't need a sin-offering for Himself. All the animal sin-offerings in the Old Testament did not really put away sin; they just allowed God to tolerate it for a while until Christ came.

8. The parts of our body (feet, hands, mouth, eyes, etc.) can be used for the service of God (which is why Christ saved you and 'bought' your body); as opposed to engaging in sinful activity.

SESSION 10: FAMILY LIFE

1. They did everything together; they taught Apollos - they used their home; they risked their lives for the apostle Paul; the Assembly met in their home - they showed generosity.

2. Altering correct priorities to do an unimportant task; saying one thing and doing another; never being satisfied; not listening or communicating; making unjustified accusations.

3. Conflicting schedules of family members - requires planning; forgetfulness, inconsistency - get into the habit; varying desire for it - encourage a respect for it; some may prefer individual study - keep it short.

4. In early years, parents need to control what children wear; as they grow older, their individuality becomes more evident and they should be given more latitude, but parents may still need to counsel as to governing principles - modesty, avoiding worldliness, respect to the body (as a temple of the Holy Spirit).

5. Subjection is a role and an attitude; it does not imply lower status or inequality; Christ was voluntarily subject to His Father (Philippians 2:5-7; 1 Corinthians 15:28); subjection brings reward (James 4:6,10).

6. Only when they are older and independent of their parents, or when their

parents' command is illegal or clearly contrary to Scripture (care needs to be exercised).

7. Personal answer.

SESSION 11: MAKING OTHER DISCIPLES

1. Nicodemus was a religious man who came with a spiritual enquiry; the Lord counselled him, based on what Nicodemus already knew, and showed him something new - that he had to be born again. The Samaritan woman had very limited knowledge and did not approach Christ. He opened the conversation very generally and proceeded to introduce her to her need for eternal life.

2. No, it means we should also always be ready for an unanticipated question. Matthew 28:19 shows that we should also take the initiative.

3. Personal answer.

4. Repentance - He made a factual statement about her sinful condition ("he whom you now have is not your husband"); Faith - He showed His knowledge of the things of God and revealed Himself to be the Christ.

5. Their attitude of discipleship should be fully evident; their knowledge of the requirements need not be very much; that is the reason for teaching afterwards; depending on their age, they should understand the implications of what they are doing.

6. All human beings are sinful and thus condemned to eternal death][God cannot overlook that sin; the judgement must be borne; the judgement could only be borne by someone who was (i) also a human being, but (ii) sinless; Christ met all the requirements; God can now save us if we accept the work of Christ for ourselves.

7. Acts 13 - Paul was invited to speak in the synagogue to Jews and Gentiles who were worshipping God and were familiar with the Old Testament Scriptures. He related everything to what they knew and showed that Jesus was the fulfilment of that; Acts 17 - Paul spoke to Gentiles who were pagans. He related the gospel to an inscription on one of their own idols, and started by explaining that there was one living God in heaven

who was their Creator.

SESSION 12: THE TRIUNE GOD

1. They are ignorant of the Scriptures; they are rebellious and independent.
2. This does not refer to Adam's body but to his essential being - having an intellect, emotions and a will, and a human spirit
3. No – God's revengefulness is not sin in that He is totally righteous; sins against Him must be avenged (but only by Him) so that His righteousness is not compromised.
4. God wanted beings who would, of their own free will, understand and appreciate the greatness of God and praise Him for it. The first creation (angels) rebelled. Humans were his second creation.
5. They are all equal.
6. It is God the Father's highest title, since it describes His dual relationship, not with us, but with Christ - as His God (as Son of Man) and His Father (as Son of God).
7. Philippians 3:21 - our bodies will be transformed to be like His glorious body.
8. a) people are confused today; Christ will make their condition and relationship with God clear; b) in the midst of lies, omissions and misleading statements, what Christ says can be totally relied on; c) He can satisfy the spiritual needs of people; d) He is the access to God.
9. God the Father - we address the worship to Him; God the Son - He is the subject of our worship; we tell God the Father about Him; God the Spirit - the Holy Spirit enables us to express our worship.

SESSION 13: THE HOLY SPIRIT (PART 1)

1. Comforter - One who encourages us; Helper - One who strengthens us; Counsellor - One who advises us; Advocate - One who pleads our case with God.
2. Behaviour such as: untruthfulness, sinful anger, stealing, unwholesome

talk, bitterness, brawling, slander, malice.

3. The fruit in Galatians 5 is the conduct and attitude of Christ. The fruit in John 15 would seem to refer to this also. It can only be produced as the disciple stays in contact with Christ, through the scriptures. John 15:7 – "if my words remain in you"; verse 10 – "if you obey my commands."

4. The Holy Spirit, to the extent we permit it, strengthens us internally - by enabling us to recall scripture, speak and act with confidence, and for our service to have results.

SESSION 14: THE HOLY SPIRIT (PART 2)

1. They are to work together in harmony, like a body (1 Corinthians 12:25). The Corinthians were reminded that they were part of the body of Christ; these principles were to function in their assembly. The various gifts were given for the building up of the body to attain the unity of the faith, that is: the doctrine of the Lord.

2. Using every opportunity to put it into practice; learning all you can about it from Scripture; observing good role models.

SESSION 15: FUTURE EVENTS

1. Judgement Seat of Christ is: for believers - not to determine if they are saved- not for condemnation but for reward for service to Christ. Great White Throne: comes over 1000 years later- is not for believers of this age- is for determination of eternal destiny.

2. Tthe nations' armies will congregate in the valley of Armageddon to prepare to attack Jerusalem (those from the east - will have crossed the dried-up river Euphrates); they will attack Jerusalem, causing havoc; the sky will darken; Christ will return in full glory with His saints to the Mount of Olives (east of Jerusalem) and lead His army who battle against the nations; He will be victorious and will capture the 'beast' and 'false prophet'; Valley of 'Har-meggiddo' (valley of Jezreel) runs east from Haifa (Mount Carmel) to south end of Sea of Galilee - was a major route

from Egypt to Damascus (the via Maris).

3. Christ will return to the earth at the end of the Tribulation (Revelation 19); when Christ returns for Christians there will be some who are "alive, who are left" (1 Thessalonians 4:15), whereas, in the Tribulation, those who do not worship the Beast will be slain (Revelation 13:15); only condition of salvation today is faith in Christ; at that time it will require resistance to the Beast; He will previously have come to the air, and we will have been caught up to meet Him, from which time "we will ever be with the Lord."

4. a) Death, crying, pain (v.4) - all put away; b) temple (v.22) - God and Christ are there in person; c) sun or moon (v.23) - God Himself is the source of light; d) impurity (v.27) - impure persons have previously been sentenced to judgement. There may also be no sea, perhaps because it separates.

5. Each one will give account of his own actions to Christ; overseers will also give account for the saints under their care; each action will be evaluated as to its merit; true motives for those actions will be revealed; each one will receive praise and reward for any good and faithful service; there will be no praise or reward for service that was of no value or for opportunities missed.

SESSION 16: THE CHURCH THE BODY OF CHRIST

1. It was planned by God before creation but hidden from men and angels until it was revealed by Christ and explained by Paul.

2. Baptism in the Spirit is a spiritual event which is done automatically by Christ at the moment of salvation; this baptism is into the Church the Body of Christ. Baptism of a believer in water is a physical event which is done by another disciple at the decision of the believer; this baptism is into the name of the Father, and the Son and the Holy Spirit. When Israel came out of Egypt, they went through the Red Sea under Moses their leader (baptized in water to their leader); they were also immersed in the cloud which would guide them through the wilderness (cf. baptized

in the Holy Spirit).

3. Refer to Topic Overview.

4. Christ is Head of the Church and has complete authority over it. Believers are all equal members (although with different functions - compare a hand and foot in a body), who are in subjection to the Head, and are expected to function in harmony with each other.

5. Under the old covenant and the law of Moses, only the Jews were the chosen people of God; the Gentiles were considered heathen aliens. When Israel rejected Christ, God set aside Israel as a nation but appealed to all people, Jews and Gentiles, in the gospel. Thus, in this dispensation of grace under the new covenant, the distinction between Jews and Gentiles has been eliminated.

SESSION 17: THE CHURCHES OF GOD

1. No apostles today (they were personally commissioned by Christ); no miraculous gifts and signs today (we have the completed Scripture); the early churches consisted initially mostly of Jews; they suffered a lot of persecution.

2. (1) Acts 11:26; (2) Acts 14:22,23; (3) Luke 12:32; (4) Acts 20:28; (5) 1 Timothy 3:2,5,15; (6) 1 Peter 2:5; (7) 1 Peter 2:9,10; (8) 2 Corinthians 6:16; (9) Ephesians 2:21,22; (10) 1 Corinthians 3:9

SESSION 18: THE HOUSE OF GOD (PART 1)

1. Read the Scriptures consistently during the week, examining yourself for unconfessed sin and looking for descriptions of the person and work of Christ. Ask God to give you thoughts to express to Him. Meditate on what you have read throughout the week.

2. Christ entered into heaven after the resurrection, on the basis of His shed blood, and dedicated an entrance for us. We now follow Him in (in our spirits), since He is there as a Man, as our great High Priest. Having examined and cleansed ourselves, we go in in our minds into the very

presence of God in full sincerity, to worship God for His Son.

3. You are no longer excluded from God's people which used to just consist of Jews. Now you are part of God's house, which is based on the teaching of Christ, as taught by the apostles. Every church of God is being built up on the basis of that teaching as an ever-increasing house where God dwells (in the person of the Holy Spirit).

4. Sin; Christ's atoning death; eternal judgment; necessity of personal faith; allegiance to the Lord Jesus; baptism; addition to a church of God; continuing steadfastly.

5. The individual believers belong to Him but their associations are not according to Scripture.

SESSION 19: THE HOUSE OF GOD (PART 2)

1. Volunteer as you have opportunity to do so; accept responsibility that is offered to you, and carry it out to the best of your ability; ask God to show you; don't give up too quickly, assuming that you don't have a particular gift.

2. Personal answer.

3. Part I is addressed to God and is intended for use in collective worship at the Remembrance meeting. Part II is for more general use, on other occasions.

4. The 1/10 tithe was a requirement in Old Testament times under the law; the amount of giving is voluntary now; however God's expectation of the tithe previously can be a guide to us today.

SESSION 20: THE PEOPLE OF GOD

1. Numbers and prosperity are not necessarily the marks of divine approval. Israel was told they were not chosen because they were the greatest, for they were the least of the nations, but for the glory of God. The Scriptures, rather, condemn people and churches who do not live up to God's standard of holiness and who constantly question and rail against

the revealed mind of the Lord.

2. Sisters are not inferior but are not permitted to take a public leadership role.

3. We are to keep separate from every association that is not of God.

4. There are 38 occurrences of the term 'in the Lord' in the New Testament. Of these, the ones that refer to what that sphere is, indicate that it is in the place where the Lordship of Christ is owned by obedience to Him, in the churches of God, under the delegated authority of overseers (see 1 Thessalonians 5:12).

5. Personal answer.

6. The definite article 'the' makes it a precise, defined thing. Fellowship with others is sharing; the Fellowship is a community where that occurs. Truth is what is correct; the Truth is the body of teaching from God, which is correct. Faith is believing; the Faith is what is believed.

7. The real key is a sound knowledge of Scripture. We do many things however, for which there are not definite 'chapters and verses.' These arrangements develop from necessity or convenience and are based upon scriptural principle where there is one, and upon the united views of men of experience. Where conditions change, of course, traditions may also change. (Men stand to pray so that others may hear and say 'Amen'.)

8. [a] Deuteronomy 27:15-26: 1 Corinthians 14:16; 1 Chronicles 16:36; Revelation 5:14 – 'Amen' is derived from a Hebrew word meaning to believe - see the word used in Genesis 15:6. By saying Amen we lend our support to the prayer or praise. [b] See praise offered with that title in Romans 15:6; Colossians 1:3; 2 Corinthians 11:31; 1 Peter 1:3; 2 Corinthians 1:3; Ephesians 1:3; Revelation 1:6. It is usually reserved for the Remembrance worship where we are coming to God in a unique way with a unique collective appreciation of Christ. In no sense should it be just a ritual form of address used as part or some sort of liturgy. It acknowledges God's high position in His relationship with Christ. [c] 1 Corinthians 14:34; 1 Timothy 2:8 [d] Tradition, but with no rule governing it. It would not be wrong for a brother to begin leading the assembly in thanksgiving at this point without a hymn being sung. [e]

Hymns which pertain to the praise of Christ to God, address God from a collective point of view and/or refer to the Remembrance have been placed in the first part of the book for convenience of the user. Generally speaking the hymns in the second part are not suitable in holy priesthood service. [f] Based on the principle that God should have His portion of praise before we take any for ourselves or give to other people.

SESSION 21: THE KINGDOM OF GOD

1. Worthy of respect, not indulging in much wine, not pursuing dishonest gain, husband of just one wife, manages his own family well.
2. Brothers gathered to consider the problem together, to find out the mind of the Lord, which they discerned by reaching general agreement.
3. Galatia, Macedonia, Achaia.
4. Make sure you understand it; ask them about it; then submit to it and support it.
5. They should give thanks and pray silently, sing the hymns together with the men, and say the Amen.
6. Personal answer.
7. Local overseers can provide a current list.

SESSION 22: FELLOWSHIP AND SEPARATION

1. Our harmony and sharing is not only with other disciples, but with God Himself - as we live in accordance with His commands and as we confess sins that we commit.
2. Becoming a believer in Christ is not the end of God's work in our lives; He intends us to be gathered together in churches of God and to function collectively there. Any other association of believers is outside this divine arrangement; Scripture doesn't provide for it.
3. Personal answer.
4. [a] - selfishness and greed; desire for sexual gratification]; [b] - pornographic material]; [c] - selfish ambition and pride.

5. They are a community (same word). An example is a university campus (one community) consisting of separate buildings (churches).
6. We would be supporting things that are not divinely established rather than seeking to reach those people for the house of God. Also, we would be exposed to wrong or different teaching (Galatians 2:18).
7. Excommunication is for the purpose that, where we have failed to bring about a change of attitude in the person while they were inside the Assembly, God Himself might accomplish it. If we have fellowship with such a person before there is evidence of repentance, we could well be interfering with the work of God. Extreme care is needed therefore.

SESSION 23: THE HISTORY OF THE FELLOWSHIP

1. e.g. convenient location, good attendance, good music, good minister, extensive evangelism/missionary work.
2. Needed Truth - for the teaching of the Word of God; Bible Studies - for the exploration of the Word of God.
3. Open Brethren - leads to diversity among churches, confusion, lack of unity; Exclusive Brethren - concentrates power in a few individuals.
4. The house of God in the Old Testament was destroyed when Israel was taken into captivity as judgement by God because of their idolatry; under Ezra, a remnant returned to re-establish a smaller version of the original; the house of God at the end of the first century disappeared because of wrong teaching; it was re-established in 1892, but smaller.
5. No, a church of God must be established as such under God's authority as part of the house of God - as a visibly united church, as part of the united elderhood.
6. That adherence to the truth of God is paramount; we must guard it; that there is a lot of human resistance to giving up human traditions to obey fully the Word of God; that we have to separate from error in order to practise truth; it's usually impossible to change it from within; that God's plan for a house among His people on earth cannot be frustrated forever.

APPENDIX A: THE COMMANDMENTS OF THE LORD

(A) GENERAL

1. **REPENT, BELIEVE AND BE BORN AGAIN** - Matthew 11:28; 18:3; Mark 5:36; Luke 13:3,5,24; John 3:7; 6:27,29; 7:37; 8:24; 12:36 Hebrews 11:6; 1 John 3:23

2. **BE OBEDIENT; BE A DISCIPLE** - Matthew 4:19; 8:22; 9:9; 10:38; 11:28; 12:50; 16:24; Mark 1:17; 2:14; 8:34; Luke 5:27; 9:23,59; 14:26 John 1:43; 12:26, 35; 13:17; 21:19,22; Romans 12:1,2; Philippians 2:12; Colossians 2:6; James 4:15; 1 Peter 2:16; 2 John 6

3. **UNDERSTAND AND ACKNOWLEDGE THE AUTHORITY OF SCRIPTURE** - Matthew 4:4; Luke 4:4; John 8:31; Philippians 1:9; 2:16; Colossians 3:16; 1 Thessalonians 5:20; 2 Timothy 2:15; Hebrews 2:1; 12:25 ; James 1:21,22; 1 Peter 2:2; 1 John 2:24; Jude 17; Revelation 1:3; 2:7,11,17,29; 3:6,13,22

4. **LOVE AND GROW BY FAITH** - Mark 11:2; Luke 12:22; John 14:4; Romans 14:5; Ephesians 6:16; Thessalonians 5:19; Hebrews 4:1; 2 Peter 3:18; Revelation 3:2

5. **LIVE BY THE SPIRIT** - Galatians 5:16; Ephesians 4:3,30; 5:18; 6:17 1 Thessalonians 5:19

6. **PLEASE GOD AND LIVE TO HOLY STANDARDS** - John 5:23; Romans 12:11; 1 Corinthians 9:24; Ephesians 4:1,14; 5:1,8,10,17; 6:10; Philippians 1:27; 2:14; 3:15,16; Colossians 1:10; 3:23; 1 Thessalonians 2:12; 1 Timothy 6:11; Hebrews 6:1; James 5:9; Revelation 3:18

7. **GIVE GOD FIRST PLACE** - Matthew 4:10; 6:33; 22:21,37; 23:8-10; Mark

12:17; Luke 4:8; 10:27; 12:5,31; 16:13; 17:32; 20:25; 1 Corinthians 7:23; 10:14; 2 Corinthians 8:5

8. **NO COMPROMISE WITH THE WORLD** - Luke 21:34; Romans 12:2; 2 Corinthians 6:14,17; Ephesians 5:7,11; Colossians 3:1; Titus 2:12; Hebrews 13:13; 1 Peter 4:2; 5:9; 1 John 2:15; 5:21

9. **PRAISE AND REJOICE** - Luke 10:20; Romans 12:12,15; 1 Corinthians 10:31; 2 Corinthians 10:17; 13:11; Philippians 2:18; 3:1; 4:4; 1 Thessalonians 5:16; Hebrews 12:28

10. **DON'T TEMPT GOD** - Matthew 4:7; Luke 4:12; James 1:13

11. **PERSEVERE, BE STRONG AND BE FAITHFUL** - Romans 12:12; 1 Corinthians 15:58; 16:13; Galatians 5:1; 6:9; Ephesians 4:1; Philippians 4:1; Colossians 1:23; 2 Thessalonians 1:4; 2:15; 1 Timothy 4:16; 6:12,14; 2 Timothy 1:13,14; 2:1,2; 3:14; Hebrews 3:14; 4:11,14; 6:11; 10:23; 12:1,12; 1 Peter 5:12; 2 Peter 1:6; 3:14,17; 3 John 4; Jude v.3

12. **ACCEPT DISCIPLINE** - Romans 13:4; Ephesians 4:22; Titus 1:11,13; Hebrews 12:5; 2 Peter 1:16

13. **TEST SPIRITS** - 1 John 4:1

14. **PRAY AND CONFESS SIN** - Matthew 6:6; 7:7; 9:38; 18:19; 26:41; Mark 14:38; Luke 10:2; 11:2,9; 21:36; 22:40; John 16:24; Romans 12:12; 15:30; Philippians 4:6; Colossians 4:2; 1 Thessalonians 5:17; 2 Thessalonians 3:1; 1 Timothy 2:1,2,8; Hebrews 4:16; James 1:5,6; 5:13,16; 1 Peter 4:7; 1 John 1:9; 5:16; Jude v.20

15. **HONOUR CHRIST** - Colossians 3:17; Hebrews 3:1; 12:2,3; 1 John 2:28

16. **LOOK FOR THE LORD'S RETURN** - Matthew 24:42; Luke 12:35,40; 1 Thessalonians 5:8; Titus 2:13; 1 Peter 1:13; 2 Peter 3:12; Jude v.21

17. **MAKE DISCIPLES** - Matthew 28:19; Mark 16:15; John 21:16

18. **GATHER TOGETHER** - Hebrews 10:25

19. **KEEP THE REMEMBRANCE; WORSHIP** - Matthew 26:26,27; Mark 14:22; Luke 22:17,19; 1 Corinthians 11:24,25,28,33; Hebrews 10:22; 13:15; 1 Peter 2:5

20. **BE CAREFUL OF WRONG DOCTRINE** - Matthew 16:6; 2 Thessalonians 2:2; 2 Timothy 1:18,19; Hebrews 13:9; 2 Peter 1:14

21. **EXERCISE SPIRITUAL GIFTS** - Romans 12:6; 1 Corinthians 12:31; 14:1,39;

Colossians 4:17; 1 Timothy 4:14,15; 2 Timothy 1:6; 4:5; Hebrews 5:12; 1 Peter 4:10

22. **PREACH, TEACH AND EXHORT** - Matthew 28:20; 1 Corinthians 14:1,39; 1 Timothy 4:11,13; 5:7; 6:2; 2 Timothy 2:14; 4:2; Titus 2:1,15; James 3:1 1; Peter 2:9

23. **ATTEND TO PUBLIC READING** - 1 Timothy 4:13

24. **DO THINGS IN PROPER ORDER** - 1 Corinthians 14:26,40

25. **SISTERS TO COVER THEIR HAIR** - 1 Corinthians 11:10

26. **GIVE TO THE LORD'S WORK** - Matthew 6:3

27. **CONFESS CHRIST; WITNESS** - Matthew 5:16; 10:32; 1 Peter 2:12; 3:15

28. **BE RECONCILED, AT PEACE** - Matthew 5:23-25,39; 7:1; Romans 12:18; 15:19; 1 Corinthians 1:10; 2 Corinthians 13:11; Colossians 3:15; 2 Timothy 2:23-25; 3:5; Titus 3:2; Hebrews 12:14

(B) RELATIONSHIPS

1. **HUSBANDS AND WIVES** - Matthew 5:32; 19:6; Mark 10:9; 1 Corinthians 7:2,3,10,12,13,17,20; Ephesians 5:22,31,33; Colossians 3:18,19; Hebrews 13:4; 1 Peter 3:1,7

2. **PARENTS** - Ephesians 6:4; Colossians 3:21

3. **CHILDREN** - Matthew 18:10; 19:14; Mark 10:14; Luke 18:16; Ephesians 6:1,2; Colossians 3:20

4. **EMPLOYERS AND EMPLOYEES** - Ephesians 6:5,9; Colossians 3:22; 4:1; 1 Timothy 6:1,2; Titus 2:9; 1 Peter 2:18

5. **GOVERNMENT** - Romans 13:1,5,7; Titus 3:1; 1 Peter 2:13

6. **OVERSEERS** - 1 Thessalonians 5:12; 1 Timothy 5:19,20; Titus 1:7; Hebrews 13:17; 1 Peter 5:2

7. **SAINTS** - Matthew 18:15-17; 25:40; Romans 12:13; 1 Corinthians 16:16; Colossians 4:9; 2 Thessalonians 3:15; 1 Timothy 2:12; 5:1,2; Titus 2:2,3; Hebrews 13:1; James 5:16; 1 Peter 2:17; Matthew 20:26; Mark 9:35,50; Luke 22:26; Romans 12:10, 16; 1 Corinthians 3:21; 10:12; Ephesians 4:2; 5:21; Philippians 2:3,5; James 1:10; 4:10; 1 Peter 5:5

8. **WIDOWS** - 1 Timothy 5:3,4; James 1:27

9. **ORPHANS** –James 1:27
10. **NEIGHBOURS** – Romans 13:9; 15:2; 1 Corinthians 10:24; Hebrews 13:3; James 2:8; 1 Peter 1:17

(C) PERSONAL CONDUCT AND ATTITUDES

1. **LOVE ONE ANOTHER** – Matthew 22:39; John 13:34; 15:12,17; 21:15,17; Romans 12:9,10; 13:8; 1 Corinthians 14:1; 16:14; 2 Corinthians 2:8; Ephesians 4:2; 5:1; Philippians 1:9; Colossians 3:14; 1 Thessalonians 5:8; 1 Peter 1:22; 4:8; 2 Peter 1:7; 1 John 3:23; 4:7,21; 2 John 5
2. **BE THANKFUL** – Ephesians 5:4,20; Colossians 1:12; 3:17; 1 Thessalonians 5:18
3. **ACCEPT OTHERS** – Luke 6:31,36; 22:32; John 13:15; Romans 12:15; 14:1, 13; 15:1,7; 2 Corinthians 1:4; Galatians 6:1,2; Philippians 2:4,29; 4:5; 1 Thessalonians 4:18; 5:11,13; Hebrews 10:24; 2 John v.8; Jude v.23
4. **SHOW HOSPITALITY** – Romans 12:13; Hebrews 13:2; 1 Peter 4:9
5. **CONTROL ANGER** – Ephesians 4:26; James 1:19
6. **DON'T CRITICIZE OR JUDGE** – Luke 6:37; John 8:7; Romans 14:3,13; 1 Corinthians 4:5; James 4:11
7. **DON'T SEEK REVENGE** – Romans 12:17,19; 1 Thessalonians 5:15
8. **LOVE ENEMIES** – Matthew 5:44; Luke 6:27-29,35; Romans 12:14
9. **FORGIVE AND COMFORT OTHERS** – Matthew 6:14; Mark 11:25; Luke 7:37; 17:3; 2 Corinthians 2:7; Ephesians 4:32; Colossians 3:13
10. **DON'T OFFEND OTHERS' CONSCIENCES** – Romans 14:16; 1 Corinthians 8:9; 10:32
11. **DON'T BE JEALOUS** – Romans 13:13; Galatians 5:26
12. **DON'T BE AFRAID OR ASHAMED** – Luke 12:4; John 14:1,27; Philippians 1:28; 4:6; 2 Timothy 1:8; 1 Peter 3:14; 5:7,8; Revelation 2:10
13. **MIND OWN BUSINESS** – Luke 6:42; 1 Thessalonians 4:11
14. **DON'T BE BIASED** – John 7:24; Romans 12:17; 1 Timothy 5:21; James 2:1
15. **DON'T BE BITTER** – Ephesians 4:31; Hebrews 12:15
16. **AVOID LUST AND IMMORALITY** – Matthew 5:28; Romans 13:13; 1 Corinthians 6:18,20; Ephesians 5:3; 1 Thessalonians 4:3,6; 1 Peter 2:11; 2

Peter 1:5

17. **DON'T BE DECEIVED** - Galatians 6:7; Ephesians 4:14; 5:6; Colossians 2:8,16; James 1:16; 1 John 3:7

18. **BE PATIENT** - Ephesians 4:2; Colossians 3:12; 1 Thessalonians 5:14; James 5:7,8

19. **BE WISE AND CAREFUL** - Ephesians 5:15; Colossians 2:18; 4:5; 1 Thessalonians 5:16,21; 1 Timothy 5:22; Hebrews 3:12; James 1:5; 2 John 5

20. **BE UNITED** - Philippians 1:27; 2:2

21. **BE GODLY AND HOLY** - James 1:27; 2:12; 4:8; 1 Peter 1:15; 2 Peter 1:7

22. **RESIST THE DEVIL** - Ephesians 4:27; James 4:7

23. **IF SICK** - James 5:14

24. **REJOICE IN PERSECUTION** - James 1:2; 1 Peter 2:21; 4:13,16

25. **DO GOOD WORKS** - Luke 6:35; 12:29; Romans 12:21; Galatians 6:16; 2 Thessalonians 3:13; 1 Timothy 2:10; 6:18; Titus 3:8; James 3:13

26. **DON'T TAKE OATHS** - Matthew 5:34; James 5:12

27. **BE GENEROUS** - Matthew 5:42; 10:42; Luke 6:30,38; 11:41; 12:33; 1 Corinthians 16:2; 2 Corinthians 9:7; Galatians 6:6; 1 Timothy 6:18

28. **DON'T STEAL** - Ephesians 4:28

29. **WORK FOR A LIVING** - Ephesians 4:28; 1 Thessalonians 4:12; 2 Thessalonians 3:12; Titus 3:14

30. **SACRIFICE** - Luke 14:33; 2 Timothy 2:3

31. **DON'T BE DRUNK** - Romans 13:13; Ephesians 5:18

32. **TELL THE TRUTH** - Ephesians 4:14,25; 1 Peter 2:1

33. **WHAT TO THINK ABOUT** - 2 Corinthians 4:18; 10:5; Ephesians 4:23; Philippians 4:8

34. **SPEND TIME WISELY** - Ephesians 5:16

35. **SING** - Ephesians 5:19; Colossians 3:16

36. **HOW TO DRESS** - 1 Timothy 2:9; 1 Peter 3:3

37. **BE AN EXAMPLE/FOLLOW EXAMPLES** - 1 Corinthians 4:16; 11:1; Philippians 3:17; 4:9; 1 Timothy 4:12; Hebrews 6:12; 13:7; 3 John v.11

38. **DON'T ABUSE FREEDOM** - Galatians 5:13

39. **WHAT TO TALK ABOUT** - Ephesians 4:29; 5:4; Colossians 3:8,9; 4:6; 1 Timothy 6:20; 2 Timothy 2:16,23; Titus 3:9

APPENDIX B: CHRISTIANITY A LA CARTE (LES HORNE)

Hebrews 11:39-40 - "These were all commended for their faith, yet none of them received what had been promised. God had planned something better for us so that only together with us would they be made perfect."

Hebrews 12:1-3 - "Therefore, since we are surrounded by such a great cloud of witnesses, let us throw off everything that hinders and the sin that so easily entangles, and let us run with perseverance the race marked out for us. Let us fix our eyes on Jesus, the author and perfecter of our faith, who for the joy set before him endured the cross, scorning its shame, and sat down at the right hand of the throne of God. Consider him who endured such opposition from sinful men, so that you will not grow weary and lose heart."

There is a book by Reginald Bibby called *Fragmented Gods* which is a socio-logical study of religion in Canada based on data collected over a substantial period of time. The conclusion, as far as Christianity is concerned, is that most of the people who claim to adhere to the Christian faith have adopted it in an 'a la carte' style, picking and choosing from the menu. They take what they like and leave what is not palatable to them.Peter Marshall in *Mr. Jones, Meet the Master* has a prayer which reads: "Give us clear vision that we may know where we stand because, unless we stand for something, we shall fall for anything."

I met the first Canadian who climbed Everest recently. You probably remember the 1978 expedition that survived tragedy to taste success. Two Sherpas and, I believe, one of the Canadians were killed. Laurie Skreslet, the man who was first on the summit, fell down a crevasse and spent days in hospital. Seven of the climbers quit and came home. He was not the best, possibly the least, expert mountaineer in the party, but desire and the few days' rest while his wounds healed equipped him for the final race to the top. He is going back to the Himalayas next year. In a couple of weeks he will go into training. It will start with a thorough cholesterol check and heart tests, and follow with measures of all the other key functions. The climb will take him beyond the limits of normal human endurance and, if his body were to fail him, it would be tragic for him and for other members of the party as well as for his wife and child at home.

Hebrews 12 talks about a race that you and I are expected to run in, and of the training and discipline that go with it. We all have our Everests, and the last mountain to climb is death. Before that there is pain, loss, disappointment, shame, struggles, rejection, and the ceaseless needs of people around us. The value systems of the culture we live in stress ease, luxury, entertainment, bigger and better appliances, more and more protection from effort and discomfort. It doesn't ring true to the picture of the Christian in training. Hebrews 12 says that we are not running a solitary race. We are in an arena and there is a huge audience. All the people that are named or described in chapter 11 are watching, and I think there are a lot more. All those who are waiting for the completion of the Body of Christ, my father, my mother, are in that huge audience that is watching and wishing for me to do well in the race.

What a strange description – "a great cloud of witnesses." If he had said "a great crowd" it would be easier to understand. 'Cloud'? All I can explain is that when Ben Johnson broke the world sprint record in Rome and became the fastest man alive, he knew that there was an audience. He sensed the crowded stadium but there were no individuals, no discernible faces. It was a great cloud of people. All that Ben could feel was the pressure of his feet against the blocks and the sound of the starter's voice. He was totally concentrating on the task, completely tuned to respond with responses that he had trained himself to use. Even then, he almost overbalanced as he came off the blocks. The witnesses are watching us but we have our own race and it isn't easy. It will take all the effort and determination we can find in ourselves, and then more.And the race is set.

We have no choice of the course. We have to run the track that He has marked. "Why are you taking me this way?" is not the question. The question is, "How am I going to run this stretch?" and "What are You training me for now, Lord?" I have two friends in Los Angeles. They are having a very hard time. No work, not enough income to eat and pay the rent, and several mouths to feed. They followed the track out there, in faith that God had something for them to do. Sometimes they must be tempted to ask, "Why?" but mostly they ask, "What do you want us to learn?"We have to learn to love exertion, to welcome demands, to push ourselves harder. We have to learn to fix our eyes on the Leader. He is running ahead on the same track.

Consider Him, it says. Study His style of running and how He handled the discipline and pain of the race. Study Jesus.It is no fun training hard, but if we don't train hard, we will not have the stamina or experience to achieve. If we want it easy and avoid the training, we are bastards not sons. We are not legitimate. Human fathers often apply discipline for their own good. They deal with their anger or anxiety or embarrassment by hurting the child. God always does it for our good. "That we may share in His holiness."Holiness. I used to avoid the word. It represented a way of dressing, an air of superiority, and absence of joy, and a sort of arid severity. Now I love it and fear it at the same time. I know now that it means separation by difference, removal from the profane. God is holy and I am so glad because if there were a hint of the profane, or any sameness to the world in Him, there would be no salvation, no escape from disaster. Everything would be doomed.Holiness means reserved for the service of God.

I, also, sharing God's holiness, am separated by difference. I am separated from the profit motive and its effect on this world because I count everything loss. I am separated from the 'me first' philosophy because I count others better than myself. I am separated from the 'I survived' attitude because every day is dedicated to His will. I am separate to serve. I want to stress the activity of holiness. I have trained for it, and am always in training. There are sick people to visit when I could be watching television. There are lonely people to share with when I could be lounging by the pool. There are people in prison, children in the street, youth struggling with life, and Jesus ran the race before us. When the tests come, and they will come, we will need all the training. It is too late to start toning up flabby muscles when the starter starts calling you to the blocks. You shall not withhold yourself. Go.

Life is always an adventure, never a drag. Never ... 'Aw, another work day.' Or, 'Another rotten day at school.' Circumstances may be difficult and experiences painful but they are all part of the achievement and necessary to it. The race goes on. There are holy days but no holidays, rest times but no vacations. Every muscle in your body and every ounce of your will power is going to be tested and the bigger and stronger you are, the more there is to test. You will need three things. Desire, single minded determination to achieve. Consider Him, copy His style, follow His strategy in the race. Faith, see where you are going even when nobody else is looking at it. You shall not withhold yourself. Go.

ABOUT HAYES PRESS

Hayes Press (www.hayespress.org) is a registered charity in the United Kingdom, whose primary mission is to disseminate the Word of God, mainly through literature. It is one of the largest distributors of gospel tracts and leaflets in the United Kingdom, with over 100 titles and many thousands dispatched annually. In addition to paperbacks and eBooks, Hayes Press also publishes Plus Eagles' Wings, a fun and educational Bible magazine for children, and Golden Bells, a popular daily Bible reading calendar in wall or desk formats.

If you would like to contact Hayes Press, there are a number of ways you can do so:

By mail: c/o The Barn, Flaxlands, Royal Wootton Bassett, Wiltshire, UK SN4 8DY

By phone: 01793 850598

By eMail: info@hayespress.org

via Facebook: www.facebook.com/hayespress.org

MORE STUDY BOOKS FROM HAYES PRESS

- Transformed by the Gospel: A Bible Study of the Book of Romans (TFS)
- The Believer's Position and the Disciple's Practice: A Bible Study of the Book of Ephesians (TFS)
- Serving Acceptably: A Bible Study of the Book of Hebrews (TFS)
- Where is God's House Today? (Alan Toms)
- Uncovering the Pattern: God's Way of Unity for Disciples Today (Keith Dorricott)
- Baptism - Its Meaning and Teaching (Brian Fullarton)
- The Deity of Christ (Brian Fullarton)
- The Church the Body of Christ (John Archibald)
- Elders and the Elderhood - in Principle and in Practice - Jack Gault
- The Breaking of the Bread - Its History, Its Observance, Its Meaning (Jack Gault)
- The Holy Spirit and the Believer (George Prasher Jnr.)
- The Kingdom of God and the Holy Nation (Tom Hyland)
- The Church and Churches of God
- The Bible - Its Inspiration and Authority
- Walking with God - Principles of Separation in Christian Life and Service (John Terrell)
- Key Doctrines of the Christian Gospel
- The Faith - Outlines of Scripture Doctrine (Tom Hyland & Jack Ferguson)
- Churches of God - The New Testament Pattern (Tom Hyland)
- A Bible Study of God's Names for His People